VINTAGE
LIVING
TEXTS

THE ESSENTIAL
GUIDE TO
CONTEMPORARY
LITERATURE

Jeanette Winterson

SERIES EDITORS
Jonathan Noakes
and
Margaret Reynolds

D0620358

Also available in Vintage Living Texts

Martin Amis

Margaret Atwood

Louis de Bernières

Sebastian Faulks

Ian McEwan

Toni Morrison

Salman Rushdie

VINTAGE
LIVING
TEXTS

Jeanette Winterson

THE ESSENTIAL GUIDE
TO CONTEMPORARY
LITERATURE

Oranges Are Not the Only Fruit

The Passion

Sexing the Cherry

The PowerBook

VINTAGE

Published by Vintage 2003

2 4 6 8 10 9 7 5 3 1

Copyright © Jonathan Noakes and Margaret Reynolds 2002

The right of Jonathan Noakes and Margaret Reynolds to be identified
as the authors of this work has been asserted by them in accordance with
the Copyright, Designs and Patents Act, 1988.

First published in Great Britain in 2003 by Vintage
Random House, 20 Vauxhall Bridge Road,
London SW1V 2SA

Random House Australia (Pty) Limited
20 Alfred Street, Milsons Point, Sydney,
New South Wales 2061, Australia

Random House New Zealand Limited
18 Poland Road, Glenfield,
Auckland 10, New Zealand

Random House (Pty) Limited
Endulini, 5A Jubilee Road, Parktown 2193, South Africa

The Random House Group Limited Reg. No. 954009
www.randomhouse.co.uk

A CIP catalogue record for this book is available from the British Library

ISBN 0 0994 3767 8

Papers used by Random House are natural, recyclable products made
from wood grown in sustainable forests; the manufacturing processes
conform to the environmental regulations of the country of origin.

Typeset by Palimpsest Book Production Limited, Polmont, Stirlingshire

Printed and bound in Great Britain by
Bookmarque Ltd, Croydon, Surrey

While every effort has been made to obtain permission from owners of
copyright material reproduced herein, the publishers would like to apologise
for any omissions and will be pleased to incorporate missing acknowledgements
in any future editions.

CONTENTS

VINTAGE LIVING TEXTS: PREFACE

JEANETTE WINTERSON

VINTAGE LIVING TEXTS

Oranges Are Not the Only Fruit

The Passion

Sexing the Cherry

The PowerBook

VINTAGE LIVING TEXTS: REFERENCE

Acknowledgements

We owe grateful thanks to all at Random House. Most of all our debt is to Caroline Michel and her team at Vintage – especially Marcella Edwards – but also to Ali Reynolds, Jason Arthur and Liz Foley, who have given us generous and unfailing support. Thanks also to Philippa Brewster and Georgina Capel, Michael Meredith, Angela Leighton, Harriet Marland, Louisa Joyner, Anna Troberg, to all our colleagues and friends, and to our partners and families. We would also like to thank the teachers and students at schools and colleges around the country who have taken part in our trialling process, and who have responded so readily and warmly to our requests for advice. And finally, our thanks to Jeanette Winterson for her work without whom . . . without which . . .

VINTAGE
LIVING
TEXTS

Preface

About this series

Vintage Living Texts: The Essential Guide to Contemporary Literature is a new concept in reading guides. Our aim is to provide readers of all kinds with an intelligent and accessible introduction to key works of contemporary literature. Each guide suggests techniques for reading important contemporary novels, and offers a variety of back-up materials that will give you ways into the text – without ever telling you what to think.

Content

All the books reproduce an extensive interview with the author, conducted exclusively for this series. This is not to say that we believe that the author's word is law. Of course it isn't. Once his or her book has gone out into the world he or she becomes simply yet another – if singularly competent – reader. This series recognises that an author's contribution may be valuable, and intriguing, but it puts the reader in control.

Every title in the series is author-focused and covers at

least three of their novels, along with relevant biographical, bibliographical, contextual and comparative material.

How to use this series

In the reading activities that make up the core of each book you will see that you are asked to do two things. One comes from the text; that is, we suggest what you should focus on, whether it's a theme, the language or the narrative method. The other concentrates on your own response. We want you to think about how you are reading and what skills you are bringing to bear in doing that reading. So this part is very much about you, the reader.

The point is that there are many ways of responding to a text. You could concentrate on the methods you might use to compare this text with others. In that case, look for the sections headed 'Compare'. Or you might want to do something more individual, and analyse how you are reacting to a text and what it means to you, in which case, pick out the approaches labelled 'Imagine' or 'Ask Yourself'.

Of course, it may well be that you are reading these texts for an examination. In that case you will have to go for the more traditional methods of literary criticism and look for the responses that tell you to 'Discuss' or 'Analyse'. Whichever level you (or your students) are at, you will find that there is something here for everyone. However, we're not suggesting that you stick solely to the approaches we offer, or that you tackle all of the exercises laid out here. Choose whatever most interests you, or whatever best suits your purposes.

Who are these books for?

Students will find that these guides are like a good teacher. They introduce the life and work of the author, set each novel in its context, explain key ideas and literary critical terms as they arise, suggest comparative exercises in a number of media, and ask focused questions to encourage a well-informed, analytical approach to reading the novels in a way that is rigorous, but still entertaining.

Teachers will find in this series a rich source of ideas for teaching contemporary novels and their contexts, particularly at AS, A and undergraduate levels. The exercises on each text have been tailored to meet the various assessment objectives laid down in the subject criteria for GCE AS and GCE A Level English Literature, and are explained in such a way that they can easily be selected and fitted into a lesson plan. Given the diversity of ways in which the awarding bodies have devised their specifications to meet these assessment objectives, a wide range of exercises is offered. We've had fun devising the plans, and we hope they'll be fun for you when you come to teach and learn with them.

And if you are neither a teacher nor a student of contemporary literature, but someone reading for your own pleasure? Well, if you've ever wanted someone to introduce you to a novelist's work in a way that will let you trust your own judgement and read more confidently, then this guide is also for you.

Whoever you are, we hope that you will enjoy using these books and that they will send you back to the novels to find new pleasures.

All page references in this text refer to the Vintage editions.

Jeanette Winterson

Introduction

Jeanette Winterson is not an acquired taste. If you like her work, you love it passionately, without reserve. Every paragraph is a poem, every phrase is a jewel. Her words will be talismans and guides, your copies of her books will be battered and worn, but the word-hoard you cherish will be burnished and pure. This is what she says in *Oranges Are Not the Only Fruit*:

> I want someone who is fierce and will love me until
> death and know that love is as strong as death, and
> be on my side for ever and ever. I want someone
> who will destroy and be destroyed by me.

If you don't like her work, you hate it. But there aren't any 'don't knows'. Even the people who've never read a line of her work have an opinion on Jeanette Winterson.

If you are part of the love brigade, and an admirer of Winterson's work, then you're in extremely good company. Madonna and Julia Roberts are fans; her books carry fulsome quotes from eminent writers and critics like Muriel Spark, Gore Vidal, John Bayley and Edmund White; she has won prizes in

Britain, Europe and the United States, and her work has been translated into twenty-two languages. Here she is again, in *Oranges Are Not the Only Fruit*:

> Romantic love has been diluted into paperback form
> and sold thousands and millions of copies.
> Somewhere it is still in the original, written on
> tablets of stone. I would cross seas and suffer sun-
> stroke and give away all I have, but not for a man.

It's been like that from the start. When Winterson's first novel, *Oranges Are Not the Only Fruit*, was published by Pandora in 1985 there was no hardback, and the print run was small. But readers loved it, told their friends about it, and it was those readers who turned it into a phenomenon, creating a huge audience who in turn established her success. The book itself is like no other, right from its opening line: 'Like most people I lived for a long time with my mother and father.' It's a deceptive beginning because it looks innocent enough until you discover – as you read the book – that the heroine, archly called 'Jeanette', is by no means 'like most people' and that these aren't her 'mother and father' either. Add to that the quirky humour, the extreme swervings back and forth between a banal everyday and a surreal vision, the inset fairy stories that increasingly take over the 'real' story, and the conviction of a prose that is poetic in its intensity, and you see why *Oranges* is the only fruit. As she says in *The Passion*: 'I'm telling you stories. Trust me.'

What is it about Winterson's work that makes it so distinctive? There are her themes for a start, which are always the same, though handled differently in her various books: boundaries, desire, love, loss. When you come to the borders of common sense, do you cross over? In *Oranges* (1985) and *The Passion* (1987) these are a young person's questions asked – and answered – with bravado and daring. *Written on the Body* (1992) and *Art & Lies* (1994) are not so swaggering, *Gut Symmetries* (1997) and *The PowerBook* (2000) are more cautious still, but the gusto and the wit and the fierce commitment are still the same. And the challenge remains the same. In *The Passion* she says: 'What you risk reveals what you value.'

But large and intense though these themes are, it's Winterson's literary method that makes her work so memorable. She uses a concrete imagery: if there is an adjective or adverb, it matches the noun or verb exactly; if there is a metaphor, it is extended on its own terms. Here is an example. Check out the idea of the traveller and the foreigner and the voyage and the way it's followed through. This is from *The Passion*:

> Travellers at least have a choice. Those who set sail
> know that things will not be the same as at home.
> Explorers are prepared. But for us, who travel along
> the blood vessels, who come to the cities of the
> interior by chance, there is no preparation. We who
> were fluent find life is a foreign language.

This technique makes for the power of the 'treasure phrase'. It's in all Winterson's books, and it's in her titles too. Look at how Winterson's titles mean much more than they say, so that they have become part of the language. How often have you heard some variation on 'Oranges are not the only fruit' used as a catchphrase? And who else has given us derivative headlines like 'Sexing the Shopping Trolley' or 'Sexing the City'? Then rhythm and assonance and association come in. In *The PowerBook* there is a rewriting of a story taken from Malory's *Morte d'Arthur*, and there's also a story about the Everest explorer George Mallory who was lost on the mountain in the 1920s and whose body was discovered there in 1999.

It's only their names that make this delicate and yet intricate connection, but it works, as we too start to make connections, follow threads.

Words are Winterson's tools and she is in love with words, trusts words, believes in words. But even if you have years of acquaintance with her fictions, there is still an essence of mystery. If you look at the interview with her, you will see that we pressed her on the meaning of a gnomic saying from *The Passion*, 'What you risk reveals what you value.' So what does it mean, we asked? In the end she says, quoting T. S. Eliot's famous reply to a reader who asked what the opening line of one his poems 'meant', 'It means, "Lady, three white leopards sat under a juniper-tree".' Point taken. It means, of course, whatever any intelligent reader wants it to mean. And readers do want it to mean something inspiring and true, because it sounds so wonderful and Winterson is a sound artist. What, then, can we make of her use of rhythm? Well, count up the syllables in some of Winterson's best-known lines and you'll find that they come out in eights. Poetry again, albeit by another name.

- I'm telling you stories. Trust me.
- The pineapple arrived today.
- Wherever love is, I want to be. I will follow it as surely as the land-locked salmon finds the sea.
- Why is the measure of love loss?

Then there are her literary structures. Winterson almost always uses the first person, which makes her stories sound immediate and directly personal, as if this is a someone confiding in you. And yet, that is set against a shape which is multiple, that has more than one strand. In *The Passion* and in *Sexing the Cherry* (1989) that structure is obvious because each book has two first-person narrators: Henri and Villanelle; the Dog

Woman and Jordan. But in two very different fictions – *Oranges* and *The PowerBook* – she makes the same shape by setting a 'real' story against a variety of other stories: the Jeanette strand and the inset fairy tales in *Oranges*; the Ali-with-married-redhead story and the inset rewritings in *The PowerBook*. In *Art & Lies* and in *Gut Symmetries* there are three first-person narrators. And even in *Written on the Body* – which might seem the simplest in structural terms – there is the voice of the unnamed and ungendered narrator set against the central poetic reverie on Louise and the body. The first line links them both: 'Why is the measure of love loss?'

Winterson likes to have more than one thing on the go. Measurement, comparison, analogy – these are her tools. That is why so many of her works are layered and work intertextually, referring constantly to other literary sources: the Bible, for instance, in *Oranges*; the romance quest in *Written on the Body*; scientific discourse in *Gut Symmetries*. Winterson describes herself using this technique as a 'grave-robber'.

But there is one source from which she steals that is very alive – herself. As you read through Winterson's work, you will see that she likes to quote her own texts. She knows how words can work like a talisman, but these icons flicker and change in their different settings. 'Time is a great deadener', said in *Oranges Are Not the Only Fruit*, is a reversal of a trite cliché. When she says 'Time is a great healer' in *Written on the Body*, it's already a quotation – but it's still being criticised as a cliché. *The PowerBook* is full of such returns and reinventions. Winterson's texts create their own image and their own mask. Here she is (or is she?) in the opening line of *The PowerBook*: 'To avoid discovery I stay on the run. To discover things for myself I stay on the run.'

Winterson says that with *The PowerBook* she has come to the end of a cycle. In some ways she has also gone back to the beginning, for the inset stories appear here, as they appeared in *Oranges*, and the story of the Muck House could be read as a rewriting of *Oranges*. Soon there will be a new book, but already Winterson has created a universe that is her own. A new world beckons. It may have different skies, different horizons, different stars, but one thing is sure. Nothing dazzles like the winter sun.

'I don't know if this is a happy ending but here we are let loose in open fields.'

Interview with Jeanette Winterson

Windrush: 14 September 2002

MR: Have you always written? When did you first start writing and what were you writing?

JW: I think I started writing before I could read because I wanted to write sermons, because I was driven by a need to preach to people and convert them which possibly I still am, except that now I do it for art's sake, and then I did it for God's sake. Being brought up by Pentecostal Evangelists meant that there was tremendous drive to go out there and make a difference, and I think that literature does make a difference. I think that that's its *purpose* – to open up spaces in a closed world – and for me, it's a natural progression which seems bizarre perhaps – from those days of preaching the Word to these days of trying to make people see things imaginatively, transformatively.

MR: So if you were writing before you were reading, do you still write in order to read the world?

JW: Yes. I write so that I'll have something to read, but I also write so that I can explain the world to myself, because writing becomes a third person – it becomes something which is separate from yourself. It's no longer you, although it's generated by you, and when it returns to you it explains things. It explains you to yourself and it explains the world. Books are always cleverer than their authors. They always contain more than the writer intended to put into them – at least they *should* – otherwise they become rather formulaic. I suspect creative writing school books contain only what is put into them, which is why they're so dreary.

MR: And when you were writing *Oranges Are Not the Only Fruit*, what were you trying to explain to yourself?

JW: I was trying to explain where I'd come from. I was trying to make sense of a bizarre childhood and an unusual personal history. And I was trying to forgive. I don't think it's possible to forgive unless you can understand, and one of the things that writing can do – that literature can do, that all art can do – is to help you understand. It can put you in a position which is both inside and outside of yourself, so that what you get is a depth of knowledge, otherwise not possible, about your own situation, and a *context* in which to put that situation, so you're no longer alone with feelings that you can't manage. People's powerlessness comes from feelings that they can't manage, and especially those that they can't articulate. Being able to write a story around the chaos of your own narrative allows you to see yourself as a fiction, which is rather comforting because, of course, fictions can change. It's only the facts that trap us. I've always thought that if people could read themselves as fictions they would be much happier.

MR: Was the present first line of the novel always the first line of the novel?

JW: 'Like most people I lived for a long time with my mother and father'? Yes, it was. My first lines aren't always written first, but they never change when I have written them.

MR: And in that particular case, it was the first line?

JW: Yes, it was.

MR: All right, what about the title? Was that yours? Or does it come from something else?

JW: Well, I don't know, because it's lost in a kind of prehistory now of conjecture and myth. It's a stupid title. It's definitely not a selling title, but it's become part of the language. Which just shows you can persuade anybody of anything if you do it for long enough. I don't know where it comes from. I can't remember how I thought of it, all I can remember is that it came out of the idea – the central metaphor of the orange – but why *Oranges Are Not the Only Fruit*, I really don't know. People often ask me to explain it, but I can't.

MR: But all of your titles have ended up becoming icons and end up getting used: *Sexing the Cherry* turns into 'Sexing the Shopping Trolley', *Gut Symmetries* has been turned into a headline, even the simplicity of something like *The Passion* gets reiterated. Why is it? Why do these titles move into a language that then becomes more widely used?

JW: I think because they are evocative and memorable. It's very important to have the right title for a book. Usually I think of my titles before I've written the book, and not afterwards. Which suggests that something has formed already, and simply needs to be written out – perhaps that is what happens. But I think it's important to have a title which means something to people, which they can remember and use as a talisman for what they've read, so that they associate the title with the content. It's not something separate from it. It's not just simply a way of labelling or tagging what you're writing – it's integral to it. It must be, I think, otherwise you end up with a book that is divorced from its title. I don't want that. I want the whole thing to work together.

MR: And yet it has a bigger, shadowing meaning behind it. Even 'oranges are not the only fruit' and the way it gets used as a proverb . . .

JW: Well, people can then play with it and use it themselves as they see fit. Journalists love to do that. Nothing wrong with that, because it gets the book about more widely than it otherwise might. I think it's pleasure in language. If you care about words, you'll want to have the best words on the front cover, won't you?

MR: *Oranges Are Not the Only Fruit* – for obvious reasons – is written in the first person, but actually the first person is your favourite mode. Why?

JW: Because it's direct. Because it sets up an intimacy which is and isn't true. People think that you're talking only to them. You're not, of course, because hopefully other people are reading the book at the same time. So there is a little trickery there. But there's also an honesty to it, because reading is a one-to-one experience. It's a direct connection between reader and writer. It's not the same as going to the cinema or the theatre. It's something that you do privately, silently, no one can see what you're doing, you're not sharing the experience and that does make it peculiarly intimate. I think that's valuable in a world where people have very little private time and space now because it sets up a virtual world of your own. And I like to make that space as close and as secret as I can. I like the reader to feel that for that time, at least, nothing else exists and they are entering a world – a bit like the Ancient Mariner, I suppose – where somebody is stopping them on their busy way and saying, 'Listen to this. Here's a story.'

The third person to me always seems rather omnipotent and remote and better left in the nineteenth century where it was done rather well. Some writers use it, but I prefer not to. And if I do use it I usually do so for the purposes of distance, to get away from the kind of intimacy I'm usually aiming for.

MR: In spite of the fact that you're using the first person, it's not monolithic, because you do tend to do this double-strand technique. Even in *Oranges* you have the first person, but then you have the fairy stories interweaving; obviously in *The Passion*, Henri and Villanelle; the Dog Woman and Jordan in *Sexing the Cherry*; even in *The PowerBook* a story, and then lots of other stories set against it. What's the strength of using this double strand?

JW: I continually break my narratives. Nothing depresses me more than seeing a page with no breaks in it. It's such a lot to read, apart from anything else. I like the spaces and the pauses that you can make. I think it's also important to offer these forceful interruptions to people's concentration, because the problem with a running narrative is that people skip. We all do. You're looking for the story. The language becomes something which simply conveys meaning, and not something in its own right. I believe it should be something in its own right, and that it needs to be concentrated on, just in the way that poetry does, without looking for the next bit of the story. Otherwise reading becomes faintly pornographic, doesn't it?

Because you just look for the next bit of excitement. So what I try to do, always, is remind the reader that they are reading. That this is something which demands concentration. It's not like watching television. It's a dialogue, and it's not a passive act. It's something which is absolutely active. And just as you would listen to a friend talking to you, so you have to listen to the book and you have to pick up its rhythm and move in the time that it creates. It's very important to get the right tempo and to get the right pace when you're reading somebody's work. Otherwise you're likely to read it wrongly simply because you're reading at the wrong speed. One way of helping people to pick up the rhythm is by this variety of form and use of language which changes as you go along. I don't do it accidentally. Everything that I do is very deliberate in this. And it is about telling a story in such way that, I hope, people will remember it.

Of course, some people find this vastly irritating and simply want to skip along and read a monolithic narrative. I feel sorry for them.

MR: At the end of *Oranges Are Not the Only Fruit* we get one of the inset 'fairy stories', as it were, with a character called Winnet Stonejar, which is like an anagram of Jeanette Winterson. Why is naming such an important topic for you? What is it about the magic of naming that interests you?

JW: Names are places where you pause. They are places where you recognise, they are places that tell you something about where you are. They're not accidental. Whether it's people or states or situations. And I like to play with names. Sometimes I don't use any names at all. Or the names change for the character. In *Written on the Body* the narrator doesn't have a name. I wanted that narrator to be a kind of Everyman. In *Oranges* the narrator has my name, because I wanted to invent myself as a fictional character. There has been some confusion around this, because people have thought, 'Well, it must be autobiography.' In part it is. Because all writing is partly autobiography in that you draw on your own experience, not in a slavish documentary style, but in a way that transforms that experience into something else. I saw myself as a shape-shifting person with many lives, who didn't need to be tied to one life. So it's not been difficult for me to use myself as a fictional character. Other writers do it. Milan Kundera does it; Paul Auster does it. Of course, when they do it, it's called 'metafiction'. When women do it, it's called 'autobiography'. Unfortunate.

MR: You've adapted *Oranges Are Not the Only Fruit* for the television. You've adapted *The PowerBook* for the stage. You've actually written a screenplay for *The Passion*. What are the pleasures of adapting your own work? Or are there any pleasures? Are there only difficulties?

JW: Yes. You give it a new life, and of course, for the adaptation of *Oranges* for the telly, I had to cut out all the fairy stories, and that was right, because the demands of television are very different to the possibilities of the fictional form. It would have weighed it down. As it was, it was three one-hour episodes, which is a lot for a book which is only 180 pages or so. But that's just because there's plenty packed in there. When you start unravelling, it becomes a different thing. Television and cinema work best with a simple single narrative stretch. It's hard for that medium to jump and to shift and to play and to move about. Not least because you have to film it. You have to endlessly set it up and take it down again. It's very cumbersome. You can do it in a single sentence with no effort at all in a book. It involves a crew of fifty when you try and do it on the screen. So I wanted it to be simple. I wanted people to be able to enjoy what it was, and then come back to the book if they were so interested and find the rest there. I never have any worries about that with adaptation. I don't think you need to be faithful to the letter. I just think you need to be faithful to the spirit. And then hope that people will be drawn to the work itself.

And of course it does take on a new life then. It's very exciting to watch it go into somebody else's hands, somebody else's life. When they change it and work with it, it's a collaborative venture, and writing's a very solitary venture. So, for somebody who has to sit on their own for a long time, it can be rather exciting to go out in the evening.

MR: Moving on to *The Passion* – can you remember what was the starting point? What was the key idea?

JW: I wanted to use the past as an invented country. So I knew I was going to land on some moment of history and rediscover it. And I also wanted to play with a double narrative. Having had a single voice in *Oranges*, I wanted to use two voices – again both in the first person – but contrasting and playing one off against the other. So it was a formal challenge for me, and it was one that I thought would work well with the material because I wanted to have two people in there who were of very different sensibilities whom we could get to know through their, initially separate, journeys which would then come together.

MR: In *The Passion* you owe most obviously – more obviously than in other places – a debt to another text, which is Calvino's *Invisible Cities*. But in other works you do use and work through other texts as well. What is it about using one text that already exists, and raiding it, that attracts you so much?

JW: All texts work off other texts. It's a continual rewriting and rereading of what has gone before, and you hope that you can add something new. There's interpretation as well as creation in everything that happens with books. But for me, working off Calvino was a way of aligning myself with the European tradition where I feel much more comfortable. That's a tradition which uses fantasy and invention and leaps of time, of space, rather than in the Anglo-American tradition which is much more realistic in its narrative drive and much more a legacy of the nineteenth century. Modernism here really moved sideways and has been picked up much more by European writers. We lost it completely and went back into something, from the thirties onwards, which was much closer to the nineteenth-century fictional form, whereas writers like Borges and Calvino and Perec wanted to go on with those experiments and didn't see modernism as a cul-de-sac, but as a way forward into other possibilities. I think we need that, I think it's got to be there. The playfulness and the challenge has to be there. We're not telling a story, we're not making a documentary. We're trying to get to some truths about people's lives, which by their very nature are myriad, fragmentary and kaleidoscopic. And I think cannot be best understood by a single narrative thread, however deftly told. For me, there's always something unsatisfactory about that.

MR: You work a great deal with cities *as characters* ... Venice in *The Passion*, Paris in *The PowerBook*, London in *Sexing the Cherry* ... Why do cities appeal to you as they come alive in this way?

JW: Because cities are living things. Peter Ackroyd has talked about this better than anybody else in his biography of London. They are not simply a collection of buildings inhabited by people. They have their own energy, energy which lasts across time, which doesn't simply disappear. It becomes layered like a coal seam. And you can mine it and discover it. So cities are very exciting. They are repositories of the past and they are places where energy is kept locked, and can be tapped, and I think if you are at all sensitive to that, you will pick it up. I used Spitalfields a lot in *The PowerBook* because that's a place where there is layer upon layer of life from Roman Britain, through Elizabethan times, the Georgian period, into the life of the fruit and veg market in the twentieth century, and now into a whole different world where it's part of the City, where it's about money. And all of these things coexist. It's not that one takes over from the other. It's rather that one is superimposed on the other and the other can be uncovered at any point. And Ackroyd is terribly good at this, both in his fiction and in his biographical writing. I think it's always a mistake to try and lock yourself into any one place or time, because it's simply not how the mind works. The mind always travels, and it travels dimensionally. And those people who say that this is unrealistic are themselves missing the point. Realism isn't simply about this day in the twenty-first century where we're alive. Realism is about all of those lives, all of those histories, all of those moments which can be collected and shaped by us. It's the whole picture that I'm interested in, not a part of it. Which is why I get rather cross when people say, 'Yes, but you don't write realist narrative.' I do. But it's the whole picture.

MR: What does 'What you risk reveals what you value' mean?

JW: Well, I don't know. Everybody likes 'What you risk reveals what you value', don't they? They say it to one another . . .

MR: What does it mean?

JW: It means . . . it means . . . 'Lady, three white leopards sat under a juniper-tree'. [Winterson is quoting T. S. Eliot. This is the first line of Eliot's poem 'Ash-Wednesday'. When an enquirer asked him what it 'meant', he made this famous reply.]

MR: What about 'I'm telling you stories. Trust me.' Should we trust you?

JW: I think writers should always be trusted because they are rather like Autolycus in [Shakespeare's] *The Winter's Tale*, rather dubious characters with pockets full of ribbons and coins and some things of immense value, and some things that are entirely worthless, and you're never quite sure what you might buy from them. You may do well, you may not. But it's the trustworthiness of the unreliable narrator, in that nobody is going to pretend that this is objectivity. Nobody is going to say, 'This is how life is.' The writer will say, 'Here's a possibility, here's a set of clues, here's a pattern which may or may not be useful to you.' And in those hesitations and gestures, I think, we come closer to a truth than in any possible kind of documentary objectivity. So we trust writers because they *are* untrustworthy, because they do not claim to have that certainty and that knowledge, but they do claim to have a map, passed down from hand to hand, redrawn, uncertain, but the buried treasure is really there.

MR: You spoke about rewriting a moment of history in *The Passion*. In *Sexing the Cherry* you also invent a language for doing that. How difficult was it to create seventeenth-century language? How did you go about it?

JW: Well, it isn't a real seventeenth-century language. It's a language which is not that of the present day. It's very annoying when you read what we might call a conventional historical novel and either everybody's going around saying 'Zounds!' and 'Aye, sir', and their cloaks are fluttering in the wind . . . or

– which is the American way – they sound exactly like we do. Which is irritating, because neither will do. I think all you can do with the past is reinvent it so that people don't feel that they are in a place that they know, because the past is not a place that we know. We weren't there. And no matter what records are given to us, what objects, what stories, what histories, we don't know, because we weren't present. So to get at the past, fiction is as likely a way of interpreting it as any. And I do think that history is a collection of found objects washed up through time, and that some of them we do hook out, and others we ignore. And as the pattern changes, the meaning changes. We are continually understanding our past in a different way because we are continually reinterpreting it and fiction does that very well. But you can only do it well if you let some freedom in for the imagination. You can't do it well if you're trying to lock yourself slavishly into your notion of the past – which will not be true anyway. Or if you're making the past into the present, but in a silly wig and a different costume.

MR: In some ways you are a writer of poetry who happens to work in prose. Do you have any technical rules for creating imagery, metaphor, figure?

JW: Well, I don't think of myself as a poet. I think of myself as somebody who tries to use poetic disciplines and align them in a narrative stretch. But what interests me is that every word should do its work. I'm not happy for words simply to convey meaning. It can if it's journalism and it's perfectly all right if you're doing a particular kind of record or memoir, but it's not all right in fiction, because fiction itself demands a vividness and a transparency which is only possible through an exactness of language. It must not be cloudy. The words themselves mustn't be muffled or people won't be able to hear them properly. Using just any word will not do. You have to be able to justify to yourself each word that you choose and make sure that it is doing its work in the sentence, and that sentence in the paragraph, and that paragraph in that part of the story. If you can't do that, then it means that some language has slipped away from you, and that language will not work on the reader, because you haven't made it work in its own right. It has to be muscular. It has to be agile and quick, it can't be sloppy. And we think that we can use words because we use them all the time, but we use words all the time in a very everyday, approximate way in order to convey our needs and wants, and that's not what fiction is. Fiction isn't approximate, it's precise. And that's why I get angry when I read things which seem not to care about that at all, because it just becomes journalism by another name, and indeed the best journalism is much more precise than quite a lot of fiction.

MR: You have said that *Sexing the Cherry* is a meditation on T. S. Eliot's *Four Quartets*. How?

JW: It's about time. It's about the nature of time, and time is one of the things that I'm obsessed with ... What it is, how it affects us, how it moves through us, how we move through it. And so I took that poem as a starting point to explore. And of course the river runs through *Four Quartets* and there's always water in my work, and the river runs through *Sexing the Cherry* – the River Thames is very important there. Just as it is in Virginia Woolf's *Orlando*. We use these things because they come, already full of meaning. It was Peter Ackroyd who said in his Dickens biography that simply to introduce the Thames into a book is to bring with it all of that weight of history which has gone before, and I was trying to do that. I was using it literally and metaphorically as a place where time could flow.

MR: At the end of *Sexing the Cherry* there is a meditation about the future, there's a reverie about what the future means. How it draws us, the city that is beyond ... What does the future mean to you?

JW: The future is a place no one can go, until it becomes the present. And the present is made up of so many tiny decisions that then become significant and cumulative. For me, it doesn't matter what the future brings, it matters how we live now, and it matters that we are conscious of the moment that we are in, and we make it vital, as we ourselves should be vital. To use the future as an escape, which is increasingly what's happening, is sad, because you lose the moment, and what fiction always does is hold you in the moment, though that moment is then endlessly expanded in a very Walter Pater-type way. You add more beats to your life by being able to concentrate completely in the present. It's the aim of all mysticism, possibly of all spirituality, to be *here now*. Very few of us can do it. The future is always luring us away and the past is always tormenting us ... the things we didn't do, the things that we long to do. But really, this is the only time we've got. And when you sit down to work, you know that fully. Because you are in the moment, you cannot be in any other moment, because either you're concentrating completely on what you're doing, or you're not doing it at all. So I think it's a great privilege for a writer because you have a freedom that few people ever experience. You really are in the place, at the moment, but that moment itself is fully expanded because you are travelling in time and in imagination to all sorts of other moments. In itself, the act of writing is proof that time is neither constant nor straited ... that it is this vast moving thing, entity, energy, that none of us can fully realise and that our only chance is to inhabit it as best we can.

MR: *The PowerBook*, in so many ways, works and reworks a lot of your themes, a lot of your ideas. What would you say your key themes are?

JW: Oh, boundaries, desire, time, identity. I suppose what the stories can tell us. I'm always trying to understand life as a story – we talked about that. But I don't know what I do next because I haven't done it. I only know what I have already done, and you can see patterns emerging, but it's very important not to get locked into them. So those themes are there, and possibly I will go on exploring them, but I wouldn't want to be a slave to them, any more than I want to be a slave to anything else.

MR: Why do you quote yourself in your work?

JW: Because all the books speak to each other. They are only separate books because that's how they had to be written. I see them really as one long continuous piece of work. I've said that the seven books make a cycle or a series, and I believe that they do, from *Oranges* to *The PowerBook*. And they interact and themes do occur and return, disappear, come back amplified or modified, changed in some way, because it's been my journey, it's the journey of my imagination, it's the journey of my soul in those books. So continually they must address one another. And you don't know that at the time. You only know that when you've done enough of them. But that's why I say it is a series, and that's also why I say it's finished now with *The PowerBook* and there has to be new beginning. Whether or not I'll go on quoting myself in this new beginning, I don't know.

MR: And when you were working on the adaptation of *The PowerBook* for the stage, did that turn it into a completely new work?

JW: No. The weighting of it changed because it had to for the things that we decided to emphasise or to drop. There had to be a narrative in that there had to be something that happened over the ninety minutes. It had to be an emotional journey. It's particularly important when you've got a finite piece of time. When you read a book you can take as long or as short a time as you like. When you go to the theatre or the cinema, the thing is going to unfold before you in the time allotted, the ninety minutes. So it's a different approach. And it was necessary to rework *The PowerBook* to fit that space. We were very conscious that it shouldn't be too long, and we wanted to wrap a moving story – the story of a love affair – around certain iconic moments, like Paolo and Francesca, Lancelot and Guinevere, the story of Mallory, and that was the choice. I think it worked well. And it was also a way of setting against each other things that are formulaic possibilities in the book, between having something which is a story that stands on its own, and a narrative that moves through the whole piece.

MR: You have a particular public profile beyond that of being a literary writer – especially through your website and through your *Guardian* columns. What's important to you about that role? Do you feel a public responsibility?

JW: I do now. I think as you get older and you carry on being published, you have to have a public role because people look to you, especially when times are difficult, for some sort of guidance or light. I think this may be a very bad thing, but nevertheless it's what happens. And I think you have to be able to speak carefully and honestly and well about the issues of your own time, however controversially, and about the thing that you do – which is, in my case, write books. I am quite happy to fulfil that role, the only thing that troubles me is that, more and more, we want other people to speak for us, rather than thinking things through for ourselves. That's the only danger. And of course people get very cross with you if you don't agree with them, or if you don't think in the way that they think. They can take that very personally.

MR: Does that bother you?

JW: No, it doesn't bother me. Because it can't bother me. I think that any public figure is going to be controversial in some way and, simply, you meet the challenge as it comes. The website is used extensively, and people argue continually with the columns or they get cross with me because I hold some view which they consider to be completely unreasonable. Sometimes they say, 'Well, now we know you think like this, we'll never read your books again.' The truth is that if we needed people to think the way that we did before we read their books, we should have to give up reading altogether. There are very few writers with whom one can agree, certainly in the past. I don't suppose for a minute that I would get on with T. S. Eliot. But I don't have to. Any more than people have to get on with me, or even like me. What we hope simply is that there will be an excitement about reading the books, because in some way it challenges or it chimes with somebody else's thinking.

MR: I know what the website does for readers of your work. What does it do for you?

JW: I do the website completely as a public service because I think I should. And I'm one of the few writers anywhere who runs a website like that. It is expensive in terms of my time, and it costs several hundred pounds a month to keep the site going. It costs a few thousand pounds a year to revamp it. And I don't get any money back for that, but I do it because I know that there are people all over the world who see the Internet as a genuine resource, and who want to know more about my work and who can't always get my work. They want to read the journalism, or think about some of the issues, and there's a message board up there now where people can talk to each other. They like that. This is the world we live in. It's no good saying, 'I won't communicate in this way,' because more and more people will communicate in that way and people want you to have a Web presence.

MR: Has it changed your attitude to writing?

JW: No, not at all. I don't think technology can change your attitude. I think it's simply something that you use or not, depending on where you live in the world and how you live in the world. The Web doesn't matter to me. What matters to me is that people should go on having creative ideas and go on producing interesting work. How they do it, and how they disseminate it is really unimportant. I don't care if books end up being electronic, or they end up being as they are now, paper between covers. What matters is what's in them, and not necessarily the form that they take.

MR: When Mark Hogarth bought your name [along with several other well-known literary names] and set up a website – apart from obvious practical reasons – why did that make you angry?

JW: It made me angry because I felt he had no right to cash in on other people's work, and he was not the best person then to be having an official site which people would assume was somehow authorised or blessed by the author in some way, and he could have put anything he liked up there, and it would have been very difficult to do anything about it. But I also felt that one has a right to one's own name. And I do in particular.

I have made my name, from nothing at all, and it belongs to me. Very little in this life belongs to you. But your name should. Especially if that's what you're known by throughout the world, and for your work. And it *absolutely* didn't belong to him. So I felt it was a kind of robbery. Which is why I was determined that he should fail.

MR: So your name's your own again?

JW: Yes. Completely.

VINTAGE
LIVING
TEXTS

Oranges Are Not the Only Fruit

IN CLOSE-UP

Reading guides for

ORANGES ARE NOT THE ONLY FRUIT

BEFORE YOU BEGIN TO READ . . .

— Read the interview with Winterson. You will see there that she identifies a number of themes and techniques:

- Childhood
- Naming
- First-person narration
- Double structures

Other themes that may be useful to consider while reading the novel include:

- The idea of history
- The theme of storytelling
- Parents and children
- Making yourself the hero of your own life

While you are reading *Oranges Are Not the Only Fruit*, *The Passion*, *Sexing the Cherry* and *The PowerBook* in detail it is worth bearing the overall themes listed at the beginning of each reading guide in mind. At the end of the detailed analysis

33

section you will find suggested contexts, which will help you to situate the novel's themes in a wider framework. The reading activities given are designed to be used imaginatively. Choose whichever sections most interest you or are most useful for your own purposes. The questions which are set at intervals are to help you relate parts of the novel to the whole.

Reading activities: detailed analysis

TITLE

CONSIDER . . .
— Think about the title of this fiction. What does it mean? What might it mean? Bear it in mind as you read and consider how it brings out the themes of the novel.

EPIGRAPHS

RESEARCH AND ASK YOURSELF . . .
— *Oranges Are Not the Only Fruit* has two epigraphs: the first quotes Mrs Beeton, the second quotes Nell Gwynn. Do some research into these quotations. Find out who Mrs Beeton was and who Nell Gwynn was. Why might it be significant that it is these two women in particular who feature in these epigraphs? Then try and find out if the quotations are real. If they are, what does that suggest about their importance as a preface to the novel? If they are not, what does that suggest about the fictionality of this text as a whole?

CHAPTER HEADINGS

WHY? . . .

— Where do the names of the chapter headings come from, and – once you've found out – are they in the right order? Why might Winterson have used these particular headings for her chapters? What effect does seeing a list like this, as the 'table of Contents', have on you as a reader? As you read through the book, remember to consult the chapter headings and explore how each one relates to the themes and events described throughout each chapter.

CHAPTER I, GENESIS
(pp. 3–17)

Focus on: openings

DECIDE . . .

— 'Like most people I lived for a long time with my mother and father.' What do you think might be odd about this opening sentence? Is it an ordinary statement? Or is it bizarre? Is it what you would expect for the first line of a novel? Compare it with other famous opening sentences to well-known novels. Examples might include:

- 'It is a truth universally acknowledged, that a single man in possession of a good fortune, must be in want of a wife.' Jane Austen, *Pride and Prejudice* (1813)
- 'All happy families resemble one another, but each unhappy family is unhappy in its own way.' Leo Tolstoy, *Anna Karenina* (1875–7)
- 'My father's family name being Pirrip and my Christian name Philip . . .' Charles Dickens, *Great Expectations* (1860–1)

- 'The past is a foreign country: they do things differently there.' L. P. Hartley, *The Go-Between* (1953)
- 'There was no possibility of taking a walk that day.' Charlotte Brontë, *Jane Eyre* (1847)
- 'It was a bright cold day in April, and the clocks were striking thirteen.' George Orwell, *Nineteen Eighty-Four* (1949)
- 'The beginning is simple to mark.' Ian McEwan, *Enduring Love* (1997)

Focus on: the Bible

ASSESS . . .

— As you read through this chapter, note how many references are made to the Bible or have a religious Christian context. In what way are these allusions used and how seriously should we take them? Are they amusing, or teasing? Keeping in mind that the chapter is called Genesis, what does it suggest about the setting and the context of the novel?

Focus on: characterisation

CONSIDER . . .

— Make a note of all the facts that you know about Jeanette's mother throughout the first chapter and consider how her character has been built up. What kind of a person do you think she is? Note how many paragraphs begin with the words 'My mother'. Who do you suppose will turn out to be the heroine of this novel? (You might like to look out for the later moment when the name of 'my mother' is revealed, and think about where else that name occurs in Winterson's oeuvre.)

ALSO CONSIDER . . .

— What do you make of the character of Jeanette at this early stage, and what facts do you know about her? What sort of person do you think her to be? How far are your opinions influenced by the fact that it is Jeanette who is telling the story in a first-person narrative? Note: While the first person in this story is called 'Jeanette', it is important to remember that this is not an autobiography, but a novel. 'Jeanette' is a constructed and fictional character and should be regarded as such while you are reading. Remember also that in the television adaptation this character was named 'Jess'. You might like to consider Winterson's motives in using these two names, but you should not make any easy connection between the writer and her characters or personae.

RESEARCH AND COMPARE . . .
— What significance might there be in the story of the gypsy and her palm reading on pp. 6–7? Why do you suppose Jeanette is attracted to the gypsy fair in the first place? Read the episode in George Eliot's novel *The Mill on the Floss* (1860) where Maggie tries to run away with the gypsies and ends up being returned home, defeated. What does this suggest in terms of a comparison between the characters of Maggie and Jeanette?

Focus on: fairy stories

REMEMBER, RELATE AND STORE UP . . .
— Read the short inset story about the princess and the moths on pp. 9–10. How does this story connect to the main story about Jeanette, her mother's ambition and her calling? What parallels can you draw? How much work are you – the reader – expected to put into this? You will find as you read *Oranges* that other similar inset 'fairy stories' appear. Remember always to relate them to the themes and the events being played out in the main story.

Looking over Chapter 1

QUESTIONS FOR DISCUSSION OR ESSAYS

1. 'Don't be fanciful Jeanette' (p. 13). Compare the play of what is 'real' as against what is 'fanciful' in the story so far.

2. How would you describe the language of *Oranges Are Not the Only Fruit*?

3. Assess the balance of the banal and the fantastical in the novel from what you've read so far.

4. Consider the importance of allusion and reference in this opening chapter.

CHAPTER 2, EXODUS
(pp. 21–48)

Focus on: the theme of incongruity

SEEK OUT . . .
— There are a number of examples in this chapter where incongruous things are set against each other. Even the opening conversation about school, or not school, juxtaposed with the potted beef sandwiches is one instance. How many can you find? What is the dramatic impact of this technique?

ASK YOURSELF . . .
— Look at the passages describing Jeanette's impending deafness. Look especially at the passage on pp. 25–6 where Jeanette tries to explain to Miss Jewsbury what has happened to her. Why is it strange that it is Jeanette who does the writing, when she is the one who is deaf – not dumb? Certainly, we can

39

accept that Miss Jewsbury must write. But why does Jeanette have to do so? Consider how the absurd and the incongruous work together in this scene.

Focus on: images and references

LIST AND ANALYSE . . .

— There are several references in this chapter to the colour orange and to oranges. There is also reference to Charlotte Brontë's novel *Jane Eyre*. Check out the places where these references have already happened and make connections with the present examples. From now on it would be worth keeping a note of the recurrence of a reference to each of these things.

RESEARCH . . .

— On p. 29 there is a reference to a poem by Christina Rossetti called 'Goblin Market'. On p. 30 there is a reference to a poem by W. B. Yeats called 'Lapis Lazuli'. Look up each of these poems and consider their place here. How do they serve to expand our understanding of the novel? Why might they be relevant to the themes, the imagery and the concerns of the novel as a whole?

RESEARCH AGAIN . . .

— Read the passage on p. 40 about Jeanette's reading of the Book of Deuteronomy from the Old Testament of the Bible. Then read that book in a copy of the Bible – the Authorised Version of the English translation commissioned by James I would be best. How does the book in the Bible relate to what is going on here? Note that Deuteronomy is 'the last book of the law'. Why is law – or an escape from law – a theme in *Oranges Are Not the Only Fruit*?

AND AGAIN . . .

— Look up some or any of the references in this chapter. Examples might include 'Suffer the little children', 'the summer is ended and we are not yet saved', the poems of William Blake, Samuel Taylor Coleridge and the 'Man from Porlock', the *Ring* cycle and Brunhilda confronting her father Wotan, Tennessee Williams's play *A Streetcar Named Desire*, or the Hollywood film *Now Voyager* with Bette Davis.

Focus on: fairy stories

IMAGINE AND RELATE . . .

— On pp. 47–8 there is the story of the emperor Tetrahedron. How does this story provide a parallel text for the 'real' story of Jeanette? And how does it relate to the story of the princess and the moths that you read in Chapter 1? Remember that you are keeping a note of all the inset fairy stories as they occur. Remember also that you need to perceive them as a source of comparison and reference – a double text to the main text. What difference does that make to your reading of the 'main' text?

Looking over Chapter 2

QUESTION FOR DISCUSSION OR ESSAY

1. 'What constitutes a problem is not the thing, or the environment where we find the thing, but the conjunction of the two; something unexpected in a usual place (our favourite aunt in our favourite poker parlour) or something usual in an unexpected place (our favourite poker in our favourite aunt)' (p. 44). Discuss the importance of the theme of incongruity in relation to the themes of the novel so far.

CHAPTER 3, LEVITICUS
(pp. 51–65)

Focus on: the chapter title

RESEARCH . . .

— Look at the Book of Leviticus in the Old Testament of the Bible. In this book Yahweh gives out 'my statutes and my judgements' (Chapter 18), so this is a biblical book to do with law and the imposition of order. Why, then, do you suppose this chapter in *Oranges* has been given this heading?

Focus on: comedy

ACCOUNT FOR . . .

— Look at the opening scene on pp. 51–3 where Jeanette's mother triumphs over 'the Heathen' next door. Work out why this scene could be found funny. Exactly which words and which combinations of words help to make a potentially banal and ordinary situation into one which is surreal and amusing? Underline these words. How much of the comic effect is achieved by the use of 'inappropriate' vocabulary in a particular situation? How does this method relate to the idea of 'incongruity' that you have already looked at?

EXAMINE THE WORDS . . .

— Read the passage on pp. 53–5 which begins 'My mother called herself a missionary on the home front'. How many words in this section are associated with missions and missionaries? What is the function of a missionary? Can you think of any missionaries in fiction? (One example is St John Rivers in Charlotte Brontë's *Jane Eyre*.) What do missionaries do today in the twenty-first century? Once you have thought about this and collected some examples, consider why this passage and the use of the language of the 'mission' is funny here.

Focus on: *the presentation of death, characterisation and narrative tone*

INTERPRET . . .

— Jeanette gets a Saturday job helping out the florist who has gone into partnership with an undertaker (p. 57). What new information are you given here that might help you to assess a) the characterisation of Jeanette, and b) the tone of the narrating voice?

Focus on: *inset fairy tales*

CONNECT AND ASSESS . . .

— Another inset fairy tale appears on pp. 58–65. How do you know that that is what it is? Think about the introduction to the fairy tale on p. 58, the kinds of characters involved and the language used. How do the events of this story connect to the 'main' Jeanette story? How do the events of this story connect to the other inset fairy stories that you have read so far?

Focus on: *perfection and allusion*

ILLUSTRATE AND EXPLAIN . . .

— Look up the words 'perfection' and 'perfect' in a thesaurus. List as many different meanings as you can. Then look at this section and the ways in which both the 'main' story and the inset fairy tale consider the applications of the words. What do you think the term 'perfection' means? There are (at least) two hidden texts in this section: the idea of the 'quest' for perfection and flawlessness might suggest the story of Sir Gawain who was the most perfect knight of King Arthur's Round Table and therefore the only one fit to find the Holy Grail. The reference at the end of the story (p. 65) to the book about how to make a perfect person might allude to Mary Shelley's *Frankenstein* (1818) and the many stage and film versions thereof

43

('this geezer gets a bolt through the neck . . .'). Look up either of these stories and consider how they might help in assessing the role and character of the notion of 'perfection'.

CHAPTER 4, NUMBERS
(pp. 69–87)

Focus on: men and women

EVALUATE . . .

— On pp. 69–75 Jeanette tries to think through what she knows about relations between men and women. How does she go about this? What references does she use? Note the fairy tales and the allusion to *Jane Eyre*. Note how her language of 'beasts' and 'pigs' is derived from stories that she has heard. What happens when that language is applied literally? How much truth might there be in all this childish and absurd speculation? Is it really so childish or so absurd?

Focus on: allusions

RELATE . . .

— There are several fairy tales mentioned in the chapter, as well as the constituent elements of fairy tales (as in Jeanette's dream related on p. 69). How does the appearance of these allusions in the 'real' part of the story help to make connections with the inset fairy-tale part of the narrative?

JUDGE . . .
— On pp. 72–3 Jeanette tells us that she has found out that
– contrary to what her mother told her – Jane Eyre did not
marry St John Rivers. She compares this discovery to finding
her own adoption papers. Judge the significance of this
moment, and bear it in mind for later.

COMPARE . . .
— On pp. 73–5 Jeanette hides in a dustbin in order to listen to
the washday chat between Nellie and Doreen. If you look at
Robert Louis Stevenson's *Treasure Island* (1883), you will see that
at one point Jim Hawkins is similarly hidden in an apple barrel
on board the ship travelling in search of treasure when he over-
hears a conversation between Long John Silver and other mem-
bers of the crew, which makes him (and us, the readers) aware
of Silver's duplicity. Compare the two passages as fictional examples of scenes where children learn about facts in life (and the
'facts of life') by eavesdropping on adult conversation.

Focus on: pink

COUNT UP AND ASSESS . . .
— Look at the passage that introduces Melanie (pp. 75–80).
How many pink items are mentioned? Why pink? Why not
orange? What might this colour coding suggest?

Focus on: the bathetic, the sublime and literary method

ASSESS . . .
— Look up 'bathos' and 'the sublime' in the glossary of literary terms. We are told in the line preceding this section that
Jeanette will fall in love 'by mistake' (p. 75). Consider how the
story of her meeting with Melanie is told. How many elements
are bathetic, how many are sublime? Does the language and
tone of the one cancel out the importance of the other?

45

Focus on: Unnatural Passions

NOTE . . .

— On p. 83 'Unnatural Passions' is mentioned for the first time in Pastor Finch's sermon. But, in fact, such things have been hinted at already. Look back over the book so far and find as many suggestions of 'unnatural passion' as you can. Make a note of each one from the beginning of the book until the end of this chapter and consider how a narrative pattern of expectation is being set up.

RESEARCH AND COMPARE . . .

— Winterson's *Oranges Are Not the Only Fruit* has a distinctively 'lesbian' plot in that a crucial element in the story is the condemnation and outcasting of Jeanette from a close social circle as a result of disapproval of her sexual orientation. But this does not necessarily make the novel an example of 'lesbian' writing. In order to think about what might constitute 'lesbian writing', read the introduction and any of the stories collected in *The Penguin Book of Lesbian Short Stories*, Margaret Reynolds, ed. (1994).

— *Oranges* is also (in some ways) a traditional novel about a young person finding their way in the world and, as such, it could be compared with works like James Joyce's *Portrait of the Artist as a Young Man* (1916) and Alice Walker's *The Color Purple* (1983).

— Another way of considering the book would be to cast it as a romance. Read Shakespeare's *Romeo and Juliet*, especially the so-called 'ball' and 'balcony' scenes in Acts I and II. Then read the description of Melanie's first attendance at Jeanette's church and what happens after that. How many points of comparison can you find between *Oranges* and *Romeo and Juliet*? Note that there is a 'balcony' in *Oranges* too.

Focus on: inset fairy tales

CONNECT . . .

— What is the connection between the short tale on pp. 86–7 and what has just happened to Jeanette and Melanie?

Focus on: narrative irony

ASK YOURSELF . . .

— 'Our family. It was safe' (p. 86). Is it? How do you know? What makes you suspect that it might not be?

CHAPTER 5, DEUTERONOMY: THE LAST BOOK OF THE LAW
(pp. 91–3)

Focus on: narrative structure

CONSIDER . . .

— This short chapter is (more or less) set at the centre of the book. Read it very carefully. Write a five-hundred-word summary of its propositions. In what ways is this perspective on the straitjacket of conventional 'history' relevant to the arguments of the novel? Note how many stories are referred to in these three pages: for instance, the Crusades, Jonah and the whale, Pol Pot and Cambodia, Atlantis, the Pilgrim Fathers, El Dorado, the eighteenth-century Grand Tour, St George, rationing in the Second World War. How many of these stories are 'real' and how many are 'fiction'? What connections can you make between them? What connections does the narrative make between them?

Focus on: the narrative voice

ASK YOURSELF . . .

— What kind of narrative voice is speaking here? Who do you suppose is speaking? What tone is adopted? How would you describe the narrative persona in this section? Is it a voice you have heard anywhere else in the novel? What elements in the language of this section make you aware of the character of the narrative persona?

Looking over Chapters 3, 4 and 5

QUESTIONS FOR DISCUSSION OR ESSAYS

1. Consider the kinds of languages used in *Oranges Are Not the Only Fruit*.

2. Analyse the juxtaposition of the banal and the surreal in the novel so far.

3. 'When I look at a history book and think of the imaginative effort it has taken to squeeze this oozing world between two boards and typeset, I am astonished' (p. 93). In what ways does *Oranges Are Not the Only Fruit* create an 'alternative' history of the world?

4. Describe a) the character of Jeanette's mother, and b) the character of Jeanette as they are portrayed in the novel so far.

5. Write an essay on the theme of the treatment of time in *Oranges*.

6. What purpose is served by the introduction of the inset 'fairy tales' in the novel so far?

CHAPTER 6, JOSHUA
(pp. 97–121)

Focus on: the title

CONSIDER . . .
— Look up the story of Joshua in the Old Testament of the Bible. When you have read this chapter through, ask yourself why this reference has been used for its title. Look back to the end of Chapter 4 and consider how the connection is hinted at in the story of the 'Winter Palace' on pp. 86–7.

Focus on: Awful Occasions

COMPARE AND CONTRAST . . .
— Jeanette describes the Awful Occasion when her natural mother came to claim her. That is followed by the story of the Awful Occasion which is the church service where she and Melanie are challenged and by another Awful Occasion which includes the ritual of exorcism. In what ways are these three Awful Occasions similar and in what ways are they different?

ANALYSE . . .
— This is now the second half of the book and Jeanette is more self-conscious as a narrator. In what ways has her self-presentation changed? What different tone of voice is adopted here?

SUMMARISE . . .
— In no more than five hundred words, jot down a summary of the events that occur in this chapter. How much 'real time' does this passage cover? How does the treatment of time in this section compare with the way it is treated in the earlier sections?

Focus on: orange

JUSTIFY . . .
— Pick out and explain the ways in which the theme of 'orange' and 'oranges' is extended here.

Focus on: inset fairy tales and dreams

CRITICALLY EVALUATE . . .
— The inset fairy stories still figure in this second half of the novel, but they sit slightly differently in relation to the 'main' story. What difference does this make to the tone of the novel and the approach that you bring to it? Why do you suppose Jeanette's dreams now appear as kinds of 'fairy tales'?

CHAPTER 7, JUDGES
(pp. 125–34)

Focus on: allusion

WHY? . . .
— This section begins with a quotation from Lewis Carroll's *Alice's Adventures in Wonderland* (1865). If you know this moment in *Alice*, then recall it; if you don't, then look it up. Either way, ask yourself why this is an appropriate quotation at this moment in the *Oranges* story.

ANALYSE THE QUEST . . .
— On p. 127 the story of Sir Perceval begins and continues on pp. 132–3. The story is based on one that you can find in Sir Thomas Malory's *Morte D'Arthur* (*c.* 1471). You might like to look this up. But whether or not you do, ask yourself why the theme of the quest is being introduced at this point. Where have you already encountered it? How does this particular story

relate a) to the other inset 'fairy stories' in the novel, and b) to the 'main' story of Jeanette's journey?

Focus on: symbols

SEARCH OUT . . .

— Look for the ways that symbols are used in this section. The colour orange and oranges are two symbols recurring here. What old functions, from the first half of the novel, are they building on? What new functions do the symbols imply?

— Another one that you might consider is the image of the rough brown pebble (p. 128) which will reappear. Notice its appearances and make a note of them. When you've collected all the references, ask yourself how many 'meanings' there may be attached to the image of this pebble.

Focus on: mother

TRACE . . .

— Jeanette begins to analyse her mother's motives and attitudes (pp. 125–6). Look out for other instances of this. How does this – critical – attitude inform and colour the novel from now on? And how does it differ from the presentation of Jeanette's mother hitherto?

Focus on: the character of Jeanette

CONSIDER AND ANALYSE . . .

— 'The plan was the most fanciful of my brilliant career' (p. 128). In what ways is the character of 'Jeanette' developing into the narrative persona of the novel as a whole?

Focus on: the title of the chapter

CONSIDER . . .

— Think about the title of this chapter. Again, it relates to a book of the Old Testament. Then work through this chapter and note down every reference to judges, judgement and judging, and consider how all this relates to the events of the novel as a whole.

Focus on: the dog

COUNT UP AND ACCOUNT FOR . . .
— Look over the whole book so far. How often is Jeanette's dog mentioned? Can you make any special connection between these moments? Are they particular or special in some way?

AND THEN COMPARE . . .
— Read Jeanette Winterson's short story 'The 24-Hour Dog' in her collection *The World and Other Places* (Vintage, London, 1998). How does the picture of this dog, and what he meant to the narrator of the story, connect to the role played by Jeanette's dog in *Oranges Are Not the Only Fruit*?

Looking over Chapters 6 and 7

QUESTIONS FOR DISCUSSION OR ESSAYS
1. 'A complicated mind, my mother had' (p. 126). Discuss, in relation to the novel so far.

2. How many symbols can you find in the novel so far and in what ways are they employed?

3. How is the balance of power between Jeanette and her mother unfolding?

4. What new roles and what old roles do the inset 'fairy tales' serve?

5.   'The quest is all.' Discuss, in relation to the novel as a whole.

CHAPTER 8, RUTH
(pp. 137–71)

Focus on: naming and the inset fairy story

QUESTION AND DEFINE . . .
— This section *begins* with an inset story about 'Winnet Stonejar'. Why is the heroine of this story called this odd name? And in what ways does this story relate to the main story about 'Jeanette Winterson'? (You might find it useful to return to the interview with the author at the start of this book.)

CONSIDER . . .
— There are long passages here about naming and what it means and how it gives and confers power. Consider the question of naming throughout the novel as a whole. Whose names do you know? What do those names mean? In what ways does 'knowing someone's name' mean that you have power over them?

Focus on: the inset fairy story

NOTE . . .
— At this stage, we go back to the story of Sir Perceval – though it overlaps with the story of Winnet. Why might this be the key inset story at the denouement of the novel?

Focus on: incongruity, the juxtaposition of the banal and the sublime

ASSESS . . .

— In some ways the pattern of the 'real' narrative in this section (pp. 144–8) returns to the literary method of the opening sections. Why might this be? In what ways is the method the same? In what ways has it changed?

Focus on: allusion

RESEARCH . . .

— '"When did you last see your mother?" someone asked me' (p. 155). This question alludes to a well-known Victorian painting by W. F. Yeames called *And when did you last see your father?* (1878; now in the Walker Art Gallery, Liverpool). Find out about the painting and why it has this question as its title. Then work out how the situation painted there relates to the events in *Oranges Are Not the Only Fruit*.

Focus on: symbols

CONSIDER . . .

— How does the idea of the thread work (p. 155)? How does this symbol relate to others that you have met in the novel, including the rough brown pebble, orange, the demon.

Focus on: returns

ASK YOURSELF . . .

— Many of the strands of the novel are now wrapped up and brought to a conclusion. How many can you trace? Look for references to names and characters, phrases, symbols and repeated phrases or words.

Focus on: oranges

COMMENT ON . . .
— Look at the last reference in here to oranges and to the summing up of this theme (p. 167). Comment on its significance here.

Looking over the whole novel

QUESTIONS FOR DISCUSSION OR ESSAYS
1. 'When the map is unrolled, the dagger is revealed.' In what ways is the tussle for power explored in *Oranges Are Not the Only Fruit*?

2. In what ways does the concept of the proverb – a short summary of a moral proposition – underlie the literary method of the novel?

3. 'Here is some advice. If you want to keep your own teeth, make your own sandwiches' (p. 93). How does this 'advice' relate to the message of the novel as a whole?

4. Winterson describes *Oranges* as a 'comforting' novel. Would you agree?

5. 'Is *Oranges* an autobiographical novel? No not at all and yes of course' (Jeanette Winterson in the introduction to the 1991 Vintage edition). What do you think?

6. 'Jeanette's mother is the true heroine of *Oranges Are Not the Only Fruit*.' Do you agree?

7. Analyse the use of intertextual methods in *Oranges Are Not the Only Fruit*.

8. Consider the treatment of colour in *Oranges Are Not the Only Fruit*.

9. Compare and contrast the novel with the 1990 television adaptation – either in the published script, or the video of the series.

10. Describe the ways in which *Oranges Are Not the Only Fruit* functions as an experimental novel.

Contexts, comparisons and complementary readings

These sections suggest contextual and comparative ways of reading the four fictions by Jeanette Winterson. You can put your reading in a social, historical or literary context. You can make comparisons – again, social, literary or historical – with other texts or art works. Or you can choose complementary works (of whatever kind) – that is, art works, literary works, social reportage or facts which in some way illuminate the text by sidelights or interventions which you can make into a telling framework. Some of the suggested contexts are directly connected to the book, in that they will give you precise literary or social frames in which to situate the novel. In turn, these are either related to the period within which the novel is set, or to the time – now – when you are reading it. Some of these examples are designed to suggest books or other texts that may make useful sources for comparison (or for complementary purposes) when you are reading Winterson's work. Again, they may be related to literary or critical themes, or they may be relevant to social and cultural themes current 'then' or 'now'.

Focus on: adaptation

RESEARCH AND COMPARE . . .

In 1990 *Oranges Are Not the Only Fruit* was made into a three-part drama for BBC television. It starred Geraldine McEwan as the mother, Charlotte Coleman as Jess and Kenneth Cranham as the Pastor. It was directed by Beeban Kidron, produced by Phillippa Giles, and Winterson herself wrote the screenplay. The production won the Best Drama Series BAFTA award that year and a number of other prizes. The video is available from BBC Enterprises and the script is available in *Great Moments in Aviation* and *Oranges Are Not the Only Fruit* (Vintage, 1999).

— Watch the drama, or read the screenplay, and consider what changes have been made to the book. What difference does a consideration of these other versions make to your perception of the book?

Focus on: allusion

COMPARE . . .

— There are several texts alluded to, revised or rewritten in the text of *Oranges Are Not the Only Fruit*. Among these are Charlotte Brontë's *Jane Eyre* (1847), Thomas Malory's *Morte D'Arthur* (c. 1471) and the Bible, as well as the fairy stories of *Cinderella* and *Beauty and the Beast*. Choose one of these and consider the ways in which the older text is used as a counterpoint to the arguments in *Oranges*. What elements are taken from the text and reworked and what might be the purpose of that process?

Focus on: orange and oranges

RESEARCH AND ASSESS . . .
— Find out about the colour orange. Look it up in a dictionary of symbols or in a book about colour. What does it signify in different cultures? Who might wear orange and on what occasion? And what about oranges? In which countries are they a native fruit? What is their special food value? In what ways might the symbolism associated with oranges and the colour orange help you to assess the character of the metaphors used in the novel?

Focus on: the first person as hero

COMPARE AND CONTRAST . . .
— Read Alice Walker's *The Color Purple* (1983). This novel also tells the story of a young girl, her trials, her difficult family situation, her coming to terms with her own sexuality and the establishment of a sense of identity. The scene and circumstances are, however, very different for Celie and Jeanette. Compare the two works. In what ways might they be similar? In what ways are they different? Look particularly at the form of each book, and look also at the narrative methods used in each.

Focus on: coming-of-age stories

CREATE . . .
— Write your own coming-of-age narrative. Make it as long or as short as you like. Write it in the first person. Ask yourself: who is my imagined reader? How do I want to present myself? Which people shall I include? How shall I shape events for effect? How shall I finish?

COMPARE . . .

— There are many novels on the theme of coming of age. You might look at Ivan Turgenev's *Fathers and Sons* (1862); or Philip Roth's *Portnoy's Complaint* (1969), which treats the theme as farce, heavy with sexual and Jewish stereotypes; or the semi-autobiographical novels of D. H. Lawrence, *Sons and Lovers* (1913), and of James Joyce, *A Portrait of the Artist as a Young Man* (1916), which describes the writer's struggle for self-expression. To compare first-person narratives in coming-of-age novels, read J. D. Salinger's comic novel *The Catcher in the Rye* (1951), a confessional, rambling monologue by a seventeen-year-old who has escaped his upbringing and is on the run in New York; or Martin Amis's *The Rachel Papers* (1973); or Hanif Kureshi's *Buddha of Suburbia* (1990), which tracks the narrator's sexual awakening and his escape from stifling suburbia.

Focus on: the construction of the writer as public property

LOOK OUT FOR . . .

— Winterson has her own website which you can contact at info@jeanettewinterson.com. There are monthly columns, notes on her reading, information about events and performances that she is involved with. There is also a readers' group site run by Anna Troberg that you can find at www.winterson.net. This provides information, reading lists and a noticeboard for readers of Winterson's work.

— Winterson writes a regular column in the *Guardian* newspaper. Look out for these articles and consider the ways in which the concerns in her novels are taken up in her journalism.

Focus on: the idea of words as characters

RESEARCH AND COMPARE . . .

— Winterson uses words as if they were characters. Look up her short story 'The Turn of the World' in her collection entitled *The World and Other Places* (1998). In particular, read the last section carefully as she plays on the idea of the 'story' as an entity that can populate and take over a whole society. Or else look at the section in her novel *Sexing the Cherry* (1989, pp. 17–19) where the words 'resist erasure' are personified and become tyrants dominating a city.

Where else in any of Winterson's novels can you find passages that make words into characters?

Focus on: adoption

COMPARE . . .

— One theme in *Oranges Are Not the Only Fruit* is the facts – and, in this case, the problems – surrounding adoption. Many children experience a phase where they imagine that their parents are not really their parents. For children who have been adopted or fostered this is actually the case, and they may or may not know anything about their real parents. Or else there may be some conflict between their real parents and their adopted parents. If you are interested in this theme you may like to read Jackie Kay's volume of poetry called *The Adoption Papers* (1991) which tells a contemporary story of the experience of realising that you are not the birth child of your parents.

Focus on: orphans

CONSIDER . . .

— We do not know that 'Jeanette' is an orphan, but certainly she portrays herself as a child alone in the world and having to make her own way. In many nineteenth century novels a convention grew up whereby the hero or heroine of the novel was an orphan. Charles Dickens's novels *Oliver Twist* (1837–1838), *David Copperfield* (1849–1850), *Bleak House* (1852–1853), and *Great Expectations* (1860–1861) all rely on this premise as Oliver, David, Esther and Pip are all orphans, with Oliver and Esther also being in the dark as to their true parentage. Why do you suppose the figure of the orphan is important in these stories of growing up and self-definition? How might any of these nineteenth century narratives of self-construction relate to Winterson's twentieth century version?

Focus on: wounds

EXPLORE . . .

— The 'Jeanette character' suffers in various ways in *Oranges Are Not the Only Fruit*. She has arrived at an acceptance of the various rejections she has experienced by the end of the novel, but there are still wounds and there are still scars. Read Winterson's introduction to Jonathan Swift's *Gulliver's Travels* (Worlds Classics Oxford University Press, Oxford 1999). Consider how her story there, based on the idea of the wound Gulliver suffers in his knee, may relate to the theme of wounding in *Oranges Are Not the Only Fruit*.

VINTAGE
LIVING
TEXTS

The Passion

IN CLOSE-UP

Reading guides for

THE PASSION

BEFORE YOU BEGIN TO READ . . .
— Read the interview with Winterson. You will see there that she identifies a number of themes:

- The idea of history
- Boundaries
- Desire
- Love
- Loss
- Memory
- Risk

Other themes might include:

- The gamble
- Magic
- Crossing over
- The city of mazes

Reading activities: detailed analysis

TITLE

RESEARCH . . .

— In the liturgy of the Christian Church what does 'the Passion' signify? Find out if you don't know already. And while you are reading think about this title and what many things it might suggest.

— Do you know what the 'Passion Play', performed every ten years in the German town of Oberammergau, is? If not, find out. Do you know why the passion flower is called that? If not, find out. Think about the meanings of the words 'passion' and 'passionate' and bear these in mind as you read the novel.

EPIGRAPH

RESEARCH AND COMPARE . . .

— The epigraph is a quotation from the ancient Greek tragedy *Medea* by Euripedes. Find out about this story. Read an English translation of the play if you can. One recent translation is by James Morwood with an introduction by Edith Hall (1998). Or else look up the story in a dictionary of classical mythology.

Medea has many incarnations: as witch or sorceress, as fratri-cide (killer of her brother), as one who betrayed her father, as lover, as exile, as barbarian, as murderess, as rejected wife, and as slayer of her own children. Bear the story of Medea in mind as you read. If you want to know more about Medea and her legends, then read *Medea in Performance*, Fiona McIntosh, Edith Hall and Oliver Taplin, eds (2000) and *Medea: Essays on Medea in Myth, Literature, Philosophy and Art*, James J. Clauss and Sarah Iles Johnston, eds (1997).

ONE: THE EMPEROR
(pp. 3–45)

Focus on: voice and characterisation

IMAGINE . . .

— Who is this speaking? He – we soon learn it is a 'he' – seems to know a great deal about Napoleon and to be intimate with the circumstances and patterns of history. How sophisticated is this narrator? Maybe you don't think he's sophisticated at all? Maybe he – or rather the text – is pretending an innocence that isn't actually there in terms of the overall narrative point of view. What special characteristics do you learn about this first-person narrator? Do you think he is telling his story from the point of view of the moment in which he is living, or from some later, considered point of view where he has more information and is more critical of the circumstances of his own past existence? Think about which words and phrases in the text suggest to you that there may be a split narrative here – in terms of time, but also in terms of the knowingness of the narrator. Remember always that this is a very intelligent and self-conscious text and that you always need to distinguish the ways in which it manip-ulates your reactions.

EXERCISE . . .
— Develop your own critical faculties. As you read *The Passion*, remember that there are (at least) three elements that you need to consider as you read and analyse any work of fiction. These are:

- Story
- Text
- Narration

The story is the sequence of events as they unfold in 'real' time. The text is the object which presents you with these 'facts' in whatever order or from whatever point of view. The 'narration' is the method in which this 'story' and this 'text' are presented. Under this heading come considerations to do with the character of the narrator. Who is he or she? Is this a 'first' or 'third' person speaking? How far can we trust them? Are they speaking in the present or from a point of view that is retrospective?
— Then there are questions to do with the ways in which the 'facts' of the 'story' and the mode of 'narration' are presented. In what order is the story told? What priority is given to which events? What symbolic value is attached to which events? Bear all these questions in mind as you read.

Focus on: colour

LIST AND ASSESS . . .
— Blue, orange, red, white, green . . . all these are colours which figure in this section and will figure again. Take each one and write down as many associations as you can for each. Once you have done that for yourself, look them up in a dictionary of symbols and do it again. For example, 'blue' is for: the Virgin Mary, Oxford and Cambridge, sadness and melancholy, heaven, the Navy, the sky, the sea, the blues . . . and what

about a 'blue' steak? Or a 'bluey' in Australian slang? Do this for any or all of the colours mentioned in this section and spin out as many of the meanings as you can in relation to the text. You will find – in the end – that not one of them is irrelevant. Keep your lists.

Focus on: women and soldiers

CONSIDER AND COMPARE . . .
— Read the five short passages on pp. 5–9. The first begins 'I wanted to be a drummer'; the last begins 'We were on our way to join the Army of England at Boulogne'. Think about the gender oppositions that are set up here. Sometimes there is a direct comparison between what women want and what men want. Sometimes there is no such comparison set up, but there is some reference that suggests we are dealing with concerns and assumptions that are often labelled 'masculine' and 'feminine'. Sort the one from the other. How many times is an accession to power (of whatever kind) associated with a 'masculine' concept? Look again at the story of the mutilated chickens battered for Napoleon's kitchen and its juxtaposition with Henri's 'availability' as perceived by the 'officer' of whose 'reputation' Henri has heard (p. 6). What links these two episodes? What links all five episodes?

Focus on: time and narrative play

READ, LIST AND TRANSFORM . . .
— Look at the short paragraph on p. 9 that begins 'The cook grabbed a chicken from the hook above his head' and ends 'He held up the chicken for our inspection.' Think about this tiny scene. We are now embarking on the story that tells about the visit of Henri and the cook and the other men to the brothel in Boulogne. But this episode is not told straightforwardly. Instead, it is interspersed with Henri's other memories. Go

through to the end of the section noting down each time we are given a passage that relates to the brothel episode. Then write out the actual events of the brothel episode in 'real' time, and briefly paraphrase all the things that happen on this occasion.

— Then go over the section again from this point on (p. 9) to the end (p. 45) and make a note of the topics covered in the other sections – i.e., the sections that tell Henri's other stories and memories and do not deal with the events in Boulogne.

— Once you have that outline, consider how each of those interspersed sections might relate thematically, metaphorically or suggestively to the scenes that are being played out in parallel in the Boulogne episodes.

Focus on: characterisation

LOOK OVER AND DESCRIBE . . .
— Read the section on pp. 10–12 that tells the story of Henri's mother Georgette. Then read on to the end of the section, paying particular attention to the stories concerning Georgette. Then write a short description of her in no more than five hundred words from the information you are given here.

— You might also do the same for another of the characters introduced in this section, choosing from: Domino, Patrick, Henri's father Claude, Henri's friend the priest, Joséphine. What function does any one (or more) of these characters serve in helping to tell you more about Henri and his attitudes and ideas?

Focus on: heroes and villains

COMPARE AND CONTRAST . . .
— Though it is Napoleon who opens the novel (p. 3) he is not significantly introduced until the passage on pp. 12–13. Look

over the rest of the descriptions of Napoleon and consider his construction as a hero in Henri's eyes. Then look over the passages in this section and consider the construction of the cook as a villain. In what ways are the two men contrasted in terms of their physical presence, their sensibilities, their appetites and their behaviour towards Henri (and others)? Are there any ways in which they are similar?

LOOK AT THE FIGURES OF CATASTROPHE . . .

— As you arrive at the story of the bungled invasion of England from p. 23 on, note down each occasion when a figure or a number is mentioned. What does this build-up of large numbers suggest a) about Napoleon's strength of purpose and role as a hero, and b) about his role as a villain?

— How are Henri's conflicting loyalties and uncertainties conveyed to the reader? What do you think of his allegiance to and love for Napoleon? How does the text manipulate you into both sympathizing with Henri's love and being critical of it?

Focus on: men and women

ASSESS . . .

— There are several stories told throughout about relations between men and women that raise questions about gender difference and social expectation. Take two examples (Georgette and Claude, Napoleon and Joséphine, the inventor from Henri's village and his wife and six children, pp. 27–8) and consider how their stories set up or subvert gendered patterns.

Focus on: writing

NOTE . . .

— 'I'm telling you stories. Trust me' (p. 13). Remember that Henri is writing a book or a diary (pp. 28–9). Remember also that he says that he cares nothing for the facts but only about how he feels: 'How I feel will change, I want to remember that' (p. 29). Bear this in mind as you read. Consider Henri as the representative of the writer. You might also look back at the interview (p. 14) with Winterson to see how she imagines the writer's role, especially in relation to the communication of the present moment to the reader, as opposed to the portrayal of the past or the future. Think also about whether or not you should 'trust' Henri as a writer, and as a first-person narrator.

Focus on: key phrases

RECALL, STORE UP AND ASSESS . . .

— Make a note of any phrases or images that you notice returning. These might include: 'I'm telling you stories. Trust me' (p. 13); 'Time is a great deadener' (p. 32); 'They say that every snowflake is different' (p. 42); 'You play, you win, you play, you lose. You play' (p. 43).

— Make a list of any phrases that attract you. Note their recurrence. Ask yourself what they mean on their own. Ask yourself what they mean in the different contexts in which you find them. Ask yourself how each occurrence relates to the others.

Focus on: the date

MAKE A NOTE . . .

— Note the date mentioned on p. 45. Remember it. You will need it later.

73

Looking over Part One

QUESTIONS FOR DISCUSSION OR ESSAYS

1. 'Soldiers and women. That's how the world is. Any other role is temporary. Any other role is a gesture' (p. 45). Discuss, in relation to this opening section.

2. Consider the portrait of Napoleon in this section and assess the significance of his role in the novel so far.

3. Compare and contrast Henri's description of his village with his description of Paris.

4. What is the function of memory in this section?

5. How reliable a narrator is Henri?

6. What are the distinctive literary and narrative techniques that mark Winterson's style in *The Passion*?

7. Why do you suppose – so far – that this novel is called '*The Passion*'?

8. Winterson says that *The Passion* focuses on a moment of 'invented history'. Discuss the ways in which she invents history in this novel so far.

TWO: THE QUEEN OF SPADES
(pp. 49–76)

Focus on: the city of mazes

MAKE CONNECTIONS . . .

— Read the section from p. 49 to p. 54. Venice is described as a 'city of mazes' where one can lose one's way, where nothing is certain and everything is always unfolding into another thing. In what ways does the emblem of the changeable and changing city reflect the characterisation of Villanelle? How is she too a 'translated' being, crossing and metamorphosing from one incarnation to another?

CONSIDER THE SETTING . . .

— There are several descriptions of Venice or Venetian scenes in this section. Make a note each time one appears and consider how the pictures are being set before you. How much of a 'real' picture are you given? And how much of it is a fantasised setting?

Focus on: naming

COMPARE . . .

— If you have read Winterson's *Oranges Are Not the Only Fruit*, look at the passage about naming that comes in the final section of that novel called 'Ruth'. You might also look at the interview included here where Winterson speaks about the power of naming. Then look up Villanelle's name. We are told that it is a French name (p. 53) and that she wears it 'as a disguise' (p. 54). Look up the form of the 'villanelle' in the glossary of literary terms. Then ponder all these things and make as many connections and significances as you can out of Villanelle's name and its importance.

Focus on: the 'philosopher friend'

CONNECT . . .
— Villanelle describes the woman who once kept 'a fleet of boats and a string of cats' and who now lives in the slime of a nook by the canal (pp. 53–4). She appears again on p. 74. Look at these two episodes and consider what the woman's role in the novel might be.

Focus on: the dates

REMEMBER . . .
— Keep a lookout for any dates that are mentioned. Remember that we have already been given some precise dates in Henri's narrative. When you have read to the end of the section, look back at Part One and see if you can work out what is happening to both Henri and to Villanelle and at what time.

Focus on: heroes and villains

CONSIDER AND RECREATE . . .
— Napoleon was a hero to Henri. He's not a hero as far as Villanelle is concerned. Write down fifteen words that describe Napoleon. Take as many as you can from this novel, but you may take others from historical sources or from what you imagine him to have been. Then write two accounts of Napoleon, each one to be no more than 100 words long and each one to use all of your fifteen words – your first account must be written from the admiring point of view of Henri, and your second account must be from the contemptuous point of view of Villanelle.

When you have done this, look over your pieces and consider – given that you have used the same fifteen words in each account – how you have gone about putting across the particular perspective of each, whether hero or villain.

Focus on: the gamble

ANALYSE . . .

— Various games of chance are mentioned or played out here. What is the larger significance of the idea of gambling and chance in the way that the images and metaphors of the novel are being unfolded? Where have you met such ideas before?

Focus on: The Passion

ASK YOURSELF . . .

— Think again about the title of the book. How does it relate to the story as it is now being played out? How might the themes and impulses of Villanelle's story connect to those of Henri in Part One?

Focus on: red hair

FIND OUT . . .

— Villanelle has red hair (p. 51). So does the woman (p. 59). Find out what red hair is supposed to symbolise. Find out which historical and fictional characters had – or were supposed to have had – red hair, and think about why this might be attributed to them. Such figures might include Mary Magdalene, Judas, Henry VIII and Elizabeth I, Anne of Green Gables, Elizabeth Siddal and Rita Hayworth, but you will be able to think of others. You might ask a person who has red hair what they think it's supposed to symbolise.

— You could also read Marina Warner's book *From the Beast to the Blonde: Fairy Tales and Their Tellers* (1994, pp. 353–86) to see what she has to say about the symbolism of hair.

Focus on: key phrases

RECALL, STORE UP AND ASSESS . . .

— If you began the list of key phrases with Part One, continue with it now. What old phrases have you noticed being repeated? What new phrases could you add to the list?

Looking over Part Two

QUESTIONS FOR DISCUSSION OR ESSAYS

1. Compare and contrast the portrayal of Venice in this section with the picture of Paris in the last.

2. 'You play, you win, you play, you lose. You play'. Discuss.

3. In what ways is Venice construed as a 'feminine' city?

4. Explore the play with the languages of image and metaphor in this section.

5. Consider the concept of 'crossing over' as it is worked through in the novel so far.

THREE: THE ZERO WINTER
(pp. 79–129)

Focus on: Henri as writer

DISCRIMINATE . . .

— Henri is still keeping his diary. This means that his first-person narrative is also a created story that is contrived in some senses. Keep a note of how this might affect the tales that he is presenting to you and the ways in which his metaphors and images are developing. Pay special attention to any repeated words or phrases that Henri may use.

Focus on: key phrases

RECALL, STORE UP AND ASSESS . . .
— Keep aware of repeated concepts. Look (for instance) at
p. 82 where Henri thinks about passion: 'You can't make sense
of your passion for life in the face of death, you can only give
up your passion.' Or else look at p. 83: 'When I say I lived with
heartless men, I use the word correctly.' Many elements in this
novel connect with others, not in an obvious way, but subtly
and allusively. Try to keep making these connections in your
head.

Focus on: allusion

RESEARCH . . .
— On p. 83 Henri mentions Ulysses and his dog. Find the
story of Ulysses's return home to Ithaca in a translation of
Homer's *Odyssey* (Book 7, lines 290–327). Then consider how
that story might relate to the themes of *The Passion* in general.

Focus on: heroes

ASK YOURSELF . . .
— What is Henri's attitude to Napoleon now? What are his
reasons for changing his mind?

Focus on: merging narratives

CONSIDER THE OVERLAPPING . . .
— Who is the *vivandière* with Patrick on p. 87? When do you
realise and how do you know? How does the story of the gam-
bler who loses (pp. 89–94) relate to the story of the affair with
the Queen of Spades (pp. 94–6)? How does that story connect to what you have already heard in Part Two?

Focus on: naming

WHY? . . .

— Why do you suppose the man that the young woman meets (pp. 97–8) is called 'Salvadore'? Who might he be? Who might she be? How does this story connect to the others you have been told?

WHO? . . .

— Have you any ideas on who the 'rich man with fat fingers' (p. 96) might be?

Focus on: the heart

WHERE? . . .

— The woman says, 'They didn't give me enough time to collect my heart' (p. 99). Where have you seen something about 'heartlessness' before? Look out for when you meet it again.

Focus on: the journey and the homecoming

ASSESS . . .

— Read the passages that relate to the journey taken by Villanelle and Henri across Europe and then the story of their arrival in Venice. How do the images of the journey and the images of home in this section connect to the episodes that have gone before where Henri speaks about 'home'?

EXPLORE THE METAPHOR . . .

— Read the section on pp. 119–22 about Henri's journey through the house of the woman in search of Villanelle's heart. How might this be linked to the journeys they have already undergone, separately or together?

Focus on: Henri as storyteller

READ ON . . .
— You will want to know what happens, but remember to think about Henri and how he is still the teller of the tale at this moment. What happens to his perspective at the close of this section?

Looking over Part Three

QUESTIONS FOR DISCUSSION OR ESSAYS
1.   How has the image of winter functioned in the novel so far?

2.   Consider the ways in which Henri and Villanelle each reverse gender stereotypes.

3.   Analyse the treatment of 'magic' in the novel so far.

4.   Winterson says that her key themes are 'boundaries, desire, time, identity'. Write on any ONE of these in relation to *The Passion*.

FOUR: THE ROCK
(pp. 133–60)

Focus on: narrative strategies

WORK OUT . . .
— Part One was in Henri's voice, Part Two in Villanelle's, Part Three was in Henri's, but with Villanelle's own stories intervening. Read over this last section and work out which parts of the narrative belong to which narrator. What is the effect of this interweaving of the two voices at this point in the story?

CONSIDER . . .

— Remember again that Henri is a writer. He is writing now, locked up in San Servolo. It is his voice that ends the book. Look back at the interview with Jeanette Winterson and consider how her portrait of the imaginative life of the writer may be imaged in Henri's. Add in considerations of: the role of memory; the play of 'voices' in the mind of the novelist; the emphasis on the present and the reworking of history; and the fact of creating something out of nothing.

Focus on: endings

IS THIS THE RIGHT ENDING? . . .

— On pp. 143–6 we discover the 'end' of the story of Villanelle and the woman. Explain how this is the 'right' ending to that story.

ASSESS . . .

— On p. 147 Villanelle says of Henri and Napoleon, 'What is more humiliating than finding the object of your love unworthy?' How might this question also relate to the ending of the story of Villanelle's affair?

CONSIDER THE TITLE . . .

— As the book draws to a close, think again about the title. In what ways is the idea of 'passion' and 'the Passion' worked and reworked here?

RESEARCH AND CONSIDER THE ALLUSION . . .

— Read the parable of the leopard on pp. 145–6. This is a revision of a story from the Greek drama of *Agamemnon* by Aeschylus (lines 717–36) which tells how a family adopted a lion and treated it as part of the family, letting it romp with the children, and eat at their hands. But one day the lion grew up and turned on the family. It had returned to its true nature. The question the Greek text raises is this: who was most to blame, the lion who acted within nature, or the family who acted outside nature? How does Winterson's (or Villanelle's) story of the impossibility of taming passion make a pattern with – and bring to a conclusion – the rest of the themes in the book?

COUNT UP . . .

— How many stories, themes and images are tied up in this concluding section? How many phrases are repeated and to what effect? Why does the novel end at New Year? And why with those last words?

Looking over the whole novel

QUESTIONS FOR DISCUSSION OR ESSAYS

1. 'The Passion is a novel about writing a novel.' Discuss.

2. Why has Henri altered the focus of his allegiance from Napoleon to Joséphine?

3. Consider the imagery of light, as against the imagery of dark, in the novel.

4. 'My heart is a reliable organ.' Analyse this statement in relation to events of The Passion.

5. Discuss the use of EITHER the theme of memory OR the theme of history in The Passion.

6. Why might it be appropriate that so much of The Passion is set in Venice?

Contexts, comparisons and complementary readings

Focus on: the city of mazes

COMPARE AND CONTRAST . . .

The image of Venice that is employed in *The Passion* is, and is not, a picture of Venice. As far as Winterson's fiction is concerned, the most important influence on this aspect is Italo Calvino's *Invisible Cities* (1972). Winterson speaks about this in the interview. Other novels and plays similarly use the image of the city to disorient and to dismay the foreigner and the tourist. Important 'Venetian' fictions might include Ben Jonson's play *Volpone* (1605–6), Shakespeare's *Othello* (1604), Henry James's *The Aspern Papers* (1888), Vernon Lee's 'A Wicked Voice' (1890), Daphne du Maurier's short story 'Don't Look Now' (1971) and Ian McEwan's *The Comfort of Strangers* (1981).
— Read any of these works and compare their idea of the 'city of mazes' with that image in Winterson's *The Passion*.

Focus on: Venice

RESEARCH . . .

— Read some art or travel books that describe the 'real' Venice. One famous example from the nineteenth century is John Ruskin's influential *The Stones of Venice* (1851–3). A well-known text from the twentieth century might be Jan Morris's *Venice* (1960). Other useful books are *Venetian Views, Venetian Blinds: English Fantasies of Venice*, eds Manfred Pfister and Barbara Schaff (1999) and Tony Tanner's *Venice Desired* (1992).

— Can there ever be such a thing as a 'real' Venice, or is our imagination of it too coloured by the cultural assumptions of the past? If you have never been to Venice, why do you have an image of it in your mind's eye, and where have you got it from?

Focus on: Napoleon and the reinventing of history

RESEARCH AND COMPARE . . .

— Read up about Napoleon and the period in history that this novel covers, i.e., 1804–25. Good books to start with might include Alistair Horne's *Napoleon: Master of Europe 1805–1807* (1979); or Christopher Hibbert's *Napoleon: His Wives and His Women* (2002).

— Work out which elements in Winterson's fiction might be based on facts, and which are fantasies. How is the balance between them set out?

— Winterson is by no means the first writer or artist to use Napoleon as if he were a fictional character. Henri 'invents' his own ideal Napoleon but this mirrors what actually happened to Napoleon's legend, as painters of history at his court set him up – through the medium of their work – as the representative of an idealised heroism and a perfected leader for

France. On this aspect of Napoleon's history see Christopher Prendergast, *Napoleon and History Painting* (1997).

Focus on: magic in literature

COMPARE . . .

— Winterson is not, strictly speaking, a writer of 'magic realism'. This term – and it is worth looking it up in the glossary of literary terms – should be reserved for the work of a particular group of South American writers including Jorge Luis Borges, Gabriel García Márquez and Isabel Allende. However, there is a strand in Winterson's work which allies her with a modernist experimental tradition that relates to the work of Virginia Woolf – in terms of her interest in time and narrative method – and to the later work of Angela Carter – in terms of her use of history and the introduction of narrative 'magic'.

— For Virginia Woolf, read *Orlando* (1928) where the hero begins as a young man living in the fifteenth century, becomes a woman in the eighteenth century and goes on living into the twentieth century. Winterson has made a documentary on Woolf's *Orlando* for BBC 4's *Art that Shook the World* series (2002).

— For Angela Carter, read her novel *Nights at the Circus* (1984) where the heroine, Fevvers, is – we are required to believe – hatched from an egg, and has wings.

Focus on: transformation and crossing over

ASSESS . . .

— If you look at the interview with Winterson you will see that she says that one her key themes is 'boundaries'. Which means that she is also interested in crossing boundaries, in transgression, in displacement, translation and transformation. Disguise of various kinds is one of the themes of *The Passion*. Most obviously, Villanelle cross-dresses as a boy, the woman wears a mask. How many examples of transgression, or transformation can you find in the novel?

— You might like to read two books on the subject. Ovid was a Roman poet whose *Metamorphoses* became hugely popular from the sixteenth century on when it was translated into English. More recently Marina Warner's *Fantastic Metamorphoses, Other Worlds: Ways of Telling the Self* (2002) is an important analysis of the idea of transformation.

Focus on: ideas about love

ASSESS . . .

— *The Passion* is a novel partly about love, or about different kinds of love. Consider how many different kinds of love there are. How would you discriminate between: romantic love, love of God, hero worship, motherly love, paternal love, brotherly and sisterly love, friendship, sexual love? How many of these are represented in *The Passion*? How does that help to explain the title of the novel?

COMPARE . . .

— Winterson says that love is one of her recurrent themes. Read her fiction *Written on the Body* (1992) which is meditation on love and loss. The opening passages of the novel race through a number of the many clichés to do with love and the way that love is expressed and spoken of in Western culture. Read this section – or read all of the novel – and consider how the theme of love is handled.

— Read Roland Barthes's short theoretical book entitled

A Lover's Discourse: Fragments (1971: Penguin, London, 1977). This work considers the various different ways in which love works and how it can be approached and spoken of with reference to a number of key works in the European tradition. As you read Barthes's sections consider how many of his refined definitions of the processes of love might be applied to Winterson's fictions.

Focus on: storytelling

NOTE AND CONTEMPLATE . . .

— In the interview Winterson compares herself and her art to the storyteller who stays the 'wedding guest' in Samuel Taylor Coleridge's poem 'The Ancient Mariner'. She also compares the nature of storytelling to the situation of Autolycus from Shakespeare's *The Winter's Tale* pp. 15 and 21. In the one case, the Ancient Mariner stays all comers, catches them with his 'glittering eye' and makes them listen to the story. On the other hand, Autolycus has about his person the glittering objects that attract and seduce. In *The Passion* we are offered both the 'glittering eye' of the inviting storyteller, and the shiny showiness of revealing many found objects. Which version of the 'storyteller' best suits your idea of either Villanelle or Henri as Winterson's storytellers in this tale? Or does each possess a mixture of both?

Sexing the Cherry

IN CLOSE-UP

Reading guides for

SEXING THE CHERRY

BEFORE YOU BEGIN TO READ . . .
— Read the interview with Winterson. You will see there that she identifies a number of themes and techniques:

- Narrative structure and method
- History
- Time
- The city
- The river

Other themes that may be useful to consider while reading the novel include:

- The construction of a historical language
- Intertextuality

Reading activities: detailed analysis

SECTION I (pp. 8–17)

Focus on: naming

CONSIDER . . .

— The opening line of the novel, 'My name is Jordan' (p. 9), sets up the importance of the crucial role names play in this novel. Refer back to the interview where Winterson talks about the importance of naming on p. 16. Before turning your attention to the body of the text, look at the epigraphs on p. 8. Even before the novel starts, the text destabilises ideas that are central to our understanding. The first paragraph focuses upon language and it establishes that the way in which we name abstract ideas, such as 'time', shapes our understanding.

DISCUSS . . .

— Get together and talk through this philosophy of language. Is this your understanding of what naming means? What do you think about the idea that we, as a community, *name* our abstract world, and that by naming it we control it?

EXAMINE . . .

— When you have considered and talked through this philosophy, turn your attention to the opening sections of the novel and their treatment of naming. Why does the 'Dog-Woman' (p. 11) name the child she finds 'Jordan' (p. 9)? Compare this with the 'Dog-Woman' – why is she so-called? What other objects are named in this section? What is the significance of the 'naming' of the object for the community?

DISCOVER . . .

— Explore the differences between the characters' 'names'. How do their names conceptually separate Jordan from his adopted mother? Does Winterson 'name' the Dog-Woman in this section?

— Extend your exploration to include the importance of naming in Western mythology. You may want to consider Genesis in the Old Testament – naming is crucial to the idea of Creation. Equally, there are many fairy tales that place naming centrally, such as Rumpelstiltskin. Explore the importance of naming in English culture. Think about ceremonies which are considered central to human life and their relationship to naming – christenings and marriage, for example – how does naming function in these rituals? Then turn your attention back to the text. How is the role that naming plays within our culture suggested in these opening pages?

— These are questions that you may want to return to as you work your way through the text. When you have completed your analysis, return to the question of naming raised at the opening of the text and think about how your attitude to the language and naming has altered in your reading.

Focus on: journeys

DETAIL . . .

— Work your way through this opening section and pick out the different journeys referred to here. Remember to bear in mind different kinds of journeys. Use the suggestions below as a starting point, but develop the list as other varieties occur to you.

- Physical
- Emotional
- Conceptual
- Historical
- Theoretical
- Mythological

EVALUATE . . .

— 'Every journey conceals another journey within its lines: the path not taken and the forgotten angle' (p. 9). When you have detailed and categorised the different types of journey, think about how the text treats these various journeys. Pay particular attention to the idea of the journey not taken as being as real as the path followed.

COMPARE . . .

— Read Robert Frost's poem 'The Road Not Taken' (1916) and compare the propositions and arguments of the poem with the arguments set out at this point in *Sexing the Cherry*.

PERSONALISE . . .

— Think about an example of a time when you remember making the choice to follow a particular route or path. Imagine what might have happened if you had taken the other 'journey'. Write a short narrative exploring that not-taken path. Look over your narrative and think about how quickly, even in your short story, you have to make choices that leave a new path untravelled. Swap stories and think about how complicated choices become when you identify the number you make on a daily basis.

RE-EVALUATE . . .
— When you have considered your own experiences in the light of this idea, refocus upon the text and explore the novel's treatment of the journey not taken. How does this idea influence your attitude to the text? Note your expectations of the narrative at the opening and update them as you work through the novel. Think particularly about the contradiction between infinite possibility and a narrative that tells *a* story.

SECTION 2 (pp. 17–29)

Focus on: language

ANALYSE . . .
— Look carefully at the treatment of 'language' on pp. 17–21. Pick out particular words and phrases that suggest to the reader a particular version of language. Use the following questions to extend your analysis:

- How does Winterson suggest that language is a physical object?
- How does the text give language substance?
- What powers does the narrator observe in the use of language in this community?

DEVELOP . . .
— Having focused upon Winterson's treatment of language, broaden your analysis to consider the text's manipulation of

physical values. For example, think about the treatment of gravity in this section. How does the novel play with our expectations about how we inhabit houses and cities?

— In order to consider this topic more fully, you may want to compare Winterson's style at this point with Jonathan Swift's *Gulliver's Travels* (1726). Look at the treatment of the Yahoos or the Houyhnhnms and compare and contrast their version of language with the account we are given of the town where 'words resist erasure' (p. 17).

Focus on: the theme of femininity

SKETCH . . .

— 'How hideous am I?' (p. 24). Read through this description of the Dog-Woman (pp. 24–5) and from the physical description you are given, try and create a picture of her. If you prefer not to draw, use pictures from magazines and newspapers to make a collage of her appearance.

COMPARE . . .

— If you are in a group compare your different versions of the Dog-Woman. Talk over contrasting images and discuss why you have made particular choices and what you are trying to represent. How, for example, did you convey the idea of her size?

— Would you describe your Dog-Woman as 'feminine'? If not, why not? Think closely about how you understand the term. For instance, what is the difference between feminine and womanly? (Note down your definition of the term so that you can accurately analyse whether or not the Dog-Woman is 'feminine'.)

— What is it about her physical attributes, as you have represented them, which makes her *un*feminine?

CONSIDER . . .

— When you have talked about your images turn your attention back to the text and think about her representation as 'unfeminine'. Look at how other characters react to her. What do their reactions suggest about her femininity?

— When you have looked closely at the treatment of the Dog-Woman's femininity at this point, keep your notes to hand so that as you work your way through the text you can update your observations.

— Come back to this question at the end of your analysis and think, overall, about how the Dog-Woman complicates a definition of femininity.

SECTION 3 (pp. 29–43)

Focus on: gender

DEFINE . . .

— 'I have met a number of people who, anxious to be free of the burdens of their gender, have dressed themselves men as women and women as men' (p. 31). Using the resources provided define the term 'gender'.

LIST . . .

— When you have written your definition, list the characteristics you identify as being either 'male' or 'female' in terms of gender. For example, is hairiness associated with the male or female gender?

— Do some characteristics fit both the male and the female gender? As your list develops think about how complicated it is to assign attributes to one column and not the other. For instance, taking the above example further, your answer might be that both males and females are hairy but one gender works hard to remove the hair.

INTERROGATE . . .

— Look over your list and interrogate the phrase 'burdens of gender'. What 'burdens' do you perceive from your list? What differences do you identify between the burdens 'men' face, as opposed to 'women'? To develop your example here, think about the pressures upon women to be hairless, the expense of beauty treatments, and how women are critiqued if they do not attempt to remove or disguise body hair.

— Link this back to the text and consider the section's discussion of gender. How do Jordan and the Dog-Woman disrupt simple definitions of gender? (You may want to look at the previous section and its focus upon femininity.)

Focus on: the theme of love

EXAMINE . . .

— Look at Jordan and the Dog-Woman's discussion of 'love' (pp. 34–43). How do they characterise 'love'? Think about the different kinds of love they identify and question – use the categories below as a starting point. (If you are not sure what the terms mean, use a dictionary and other resources to define them.)

- Familial
- Romantic
- Platonic
- Physical
- Religious

Which, if any, of the kinds of love you have identified do Jordan and the Dog-Woman regard positively?

REFLECT . . .

— In pairs, work through your analysis. Reflect upon your

attitude to the versions of love that you are studying. How do they mirror, or complicate, your understandings of different kinds of 'love'?
— Focus particularly on the points at which your attitude to 'love' diverges from the text. Write an account that explains your perception of 'love' as you understand it. Use the text to locate your argument. Show what you disagree with and why.

Looking over Sections 1–3

QUESTIONS FOR DISCUSSION OR ESSAYS
1. Compare and contrast the characters of Jordan and the Dog-Woman.

2. In what ways does Winterson create a 'fake' language for the seventeenth century?

3. 'In my petticoats I was a traveller in a foreign country' (p. 31). Consider the treatment of the themes of transformation and disguise in Sexing the Cherry.

4. Describe and account for the imagery associated with fruit and growing things in Sexing the Cherry.

5. In what ways might the tale of the house that 'celebrates ceilings but denies floors' act as a metaphor for the construction of Winterson's fiction?

6. Analyse the image of the journey in Sexing the Cherry.

7. In what ways does this book 'break the mould of history'?

THE STORY OF THE TWELVE DANCING PRINCESSES
(pp. 47–60)

Focus on: fairy tale

REMEMBER . . .

— Take some time to remember the fairy tales that were your childhood narratives. Sketch out their plots and characterisations. What elements do you still consider to be crucial to them?

COMBINE . . .

— Taking your sketches of the fairy tales that are familiar, examine this section. Does it fit your model – is this a fairy tale? In what ways does it conform structurally and thematically to your expectations? At what points does it diverge from your model? You may want to extend this analysis to the text as a whole. Can this novel be read as a fairy tale?

THEORISE . . .

— Having produced a working model for the fairy tale which you have applied, work in pairs to formalise your model. What rules do we have for fairy tales? Think about plot and characterisation, but more importantly, focus on the themes we demand from these stories. Are they different depending upon the gender of the protagonist?

Focus on: patriarchy

DEFINE . . .

— Find out what 'patriarchy' means. Work as a group so that you establish clearly, for example, what patriarchal power is.

'Patriarchy' is a key term in much contemporary thought.

Feminist theory is sophisticated and diverse, and sometimes even contradictory, but the idea of patriarchal power is important to forming an understanding of much of it.

IDENTIFY . . .
— Now that you are happy with the term, think about the model of patriarchal society you are presented with in this fairy story. Look at how the different forms of power and influence are exercised over the sisters. Tease them out and pay attention to what it means to control an individual, not just physically, but emotionally, financially, psychologically and sexually. How are these different forms of control played out in this narrative?

INTERROGATE . . .
— When you have closely analysed the idea of patriarchy and its power, interrogate the framework in which it occurs. Use the following statement as a starting point for a discussion or as an essay: 'Marriage is a patriarchal institution – it guarantees control and the subordination of women even before it is abused.'

INTERLINK AND REASSESS . . .
— Go back to the first exercise in this section, which focuses on fairy tales. Combine your analysis of the fairy-tale narrative with your understanding of patriarchy to answer the following questions.

- Did you identify marriage as a central thematic concern in fairy tales? (*Cinderella, Rapunzel*)
- Is it of equal importance to fairy tales with male protagonists? (*Jack and the Beanstalk*)
- How is female independence treated in fairy tales? (*Little Red Riding Hood, Goldilocks*)

QUESTION . . .
— Are fairy tales patriarchal narratives? If you want to consider the question with reference to other narratives, authors such as Angela Carter address the patriarchal nature of fairy tales. Her collection of short stories called *The Bloody Chamber* (1979) would be a good place to start, or else look at Emma Donoghue's *Kissing the Witch* (1997).

Focus on: allusion

SEARCH AND COMPARE . . .
— The second and the third story here begin with reference to other texts. 'That's my last husband painted on the wall' (p. 49) alludes to Robert Browning's poem 'My Last Duchess', and 'He walked in beauty' (p. 50) is a misquotation of the first line of a poem by Byron. Look up each of these poems and consider the ways in which Winterson has 'rewritten' them.

Looking over The Story of the Twelve Dancing Princesses

QUESTIONS FOR DISCUSSION OR ESSAYS
1. 'The revision of a well-known fairy tale makes not one new story, but two in that it re-writes the old.' Discuss.

2. Assess the ways in which relations between men and women are set out in these fairy stories.

3. 'Repetition makes a learning space for new ideas.' How does the telling of eleven stories – alike but different – make demands on the reader?

4. What is the effect of the fact that the story of the Twelfth princess is missing?

1649
SECTION 1 (pp. 63–72)

Focus on: historical context

RESEARCH . . .

— This section features the Dog-Woman's account of the English Civil War, concentrating on the trial and execution of Charles I. Using the resources provided, and with the help of your teacher or group leader, research the historical context for the story you are told. You may want to assign a question to each member of your group or class and then pool your research.

- Find out who the Puritans and the Cavaliers were.
- What values did the opposing sides represent?
- How did the Civil War impact upon the public – were they generally unaffected as the Dog-Woman maintains?
- Where did the trial of the King take place?
- On what date was Charles I executed?
- Why did Cromwell seek to have the King executed?
- For how long did Cromwell rule England and what are the things for which that period is most famous?

REASSESS . . .

— Reread the account of the Charles I trial and execution. How does your greater understanding of the historical context affect your reading of the novel?

Focus on: tone and style

CONTRAST . . .

— Focus particularly on the account of Fortunata (p. 72). Look closely at the description of her school and contrast it, in terms of tone and style, with the previous section.

— Think about why this entire page is set in italics. How close is it to the centre of the text? Why is it placed at this point? Who narrates this passage? Where is the school located and what time is this story set in? Think about how this contrasts with the close historical location of the previous narrative.

IDENTIFY . . .

— When you have contrasted the two narratives, identify what role you think this italicised section plays. What themes does it establish and highlight? How does it help to frame the novel (think about beginning–middle–end)? How does the narrator of this narrative differ from Jordan and the Dog-Woman? Is this the only time we encounter this narrative voice?

1649
SECTION 2 (pp. 73–83)

Focus on: positive versus negative emotions

CONCEPTUALISE . . .

— The novel focuses once again here upon the idea of love. Think about how the idea of love as a 'plague' (p. 73) contrasts with our common understanding of love as a positive emotion. (You may want to look back at Section 3 of the opening segment of the novel that focuses specifically on the idea of 'love'.)

— Look carefully at the text's treatment of love as a potentially lethal desire, and pick out the words and phrases Winterson employs to construct this negative version of 'love'.

CHARACTERISE . . .

— Use your close reading to produce an analysis of love as a negative emotion. Take the specific words you identified, such as 'plague' (p.73), 'passion' (pp. 73–4), 'lust' (p. 77) or 'epidemic' (p. 78), and think about the consequences of associating physical responses with disease – how does this narrative define 'love' (p. 78) negatively?

EXPLORE . . .
— Look over your characterisation; how does it complicate our fundamentally optimistic view of love? Talk over your responses to this version of 'love'. Is the definition of love you are presented with here reinforced at other points in the novel?

Focus on: truth versus lies

CONSIDER . . .
— Concentrate your attention upon the end of the section (pp. 81–3) and assess the novel's treatment of the idea of truth. Is the idea of the 'truth' reinforced as a simple concept here?
— Look at the section entitled 'THE FLAT EARTH THEORY' (p. 81). How does Winterson undermine the notion that there is a clear line between the 'truth' and 'lies'?

COMPLICATE . . .
— In small groups, work together to construct a definition of what a 'lie' is, then write your collective definition. Then take each of the 'lies' listed at the end of the section (p. 83) and debate whether or not they meet your definition of a 'lie'. If the lie you are discussing seems very abstract, try to think of examples which can be more easily discussed. (You may want to choose one of the lies and come together at the end of your session to pool your responses.)

ASSESS . . .
— How has your debate about what a 'lie' is altered your understanding of 'truth'? Has it become a more complicated idea?
— As you work your way through the novel, think about how your complication of the distinction between the truth and lies informs your readings.

1649
SECTION 3 (pp. 83–9)

Focus on: the theme of perversion

JOT DOWN . . .
— Before embarking on a close reading, spend a few minutes jotting down as many different meanings for 'perversion' as you can. Sexual perversion tends to predominate but when else do we talk about someone or thing being perverted? What do we use the term to suggest? Using the list below to stimulate your ideas, consider whether these words are all interchangeable with the verb 'to pervert'. How do they convey different understandings of the word?

- Distort
- Manipulate
- Misrepresent
- Lead astray
- Turn aside
- Apostatise

EXAMINE . . .
— Tease out the different kinds of perversion the Dog-Woman discusses in this section. As part of your analysis,

remember to consider the idea of a perverted morality and a manipulation of religious values, or 'apostasy'.

EXTEND . . .

— Drawing upon your thoughts about perversion, concentrate your analysis of this section upon the phrase 'to pervert the course of justice'.

— Explore how the different characters, encountered by the reader in this segment of the narrative, attempt to pervert the course of justice.

QUESTION . . .

● Which character's moral code do you most sympathise with, and *why*?

OR

● Which character represents justice? Are they avenging its distortion in other characters?

1649
SECTION 4 (pp. 89–103)

Focus on: the theme of time and memory

COUNT . . .

— Look at Winterson's account of time in this section. How many instances are there of the word 'time'? Note down how it is employed: is it alone, or part of a phrase 'in time' (p. 96)?

ASSESS . . .

— Either alone or in pairs, think about Winterson's employment of 'time'. How does it dominate this section of the narrative? As well as examining the use of the word itself, think about other words which mark the passage of time, such as 'history' (p. 97) or the verb to 'wait' (p. 103).

DISCUSS . . .
— Language for conveying time saturates this part of the novel. Discuss the centrality of time here. How does the language reflect the thematic concerns of the novel at this point?

Focus on: images

DISCOVER . . .
— The text refers to two paintings (pp. 92, 100). Find out about these pictures. You will need to establish who they are by. Why do you think Winterson deliberately selected these pictures? How do the paintings suggest the concerns of the text?

DESCRIBE . . .
— After finding and studying the paintings, write your own short descriptions and compare them to the text. What is it that seems to you most important in the pictures? Does the difference in your descriptions suggest a different picture?

LINK AND DEVELOP . . .
— Turn your attention back to the text and read the section while thinking about the other images Winterson constructs here. Are the memories images? Look at her discussion of 'God'. Does she present us with an image? Is God given a gender here?
— Consider the employment of images here, and think about the images we bring to our readings? Does our cultural baggage mean that we have an image of 'God' before we even begin to read?

1649
SECTION 5 (pp. 104–9)

Focus on: the exotic and the natural

BROWSE . . .

— 'The pineapple arrived today' (p. 104). The novel is concerned with the idea of the exotic – this is clear both from the treatment of the pineapple here and Jordan's encounter with a banana at the opening of the novel.

— The next time you are in a supermarket look at the selection of fruit and vegetables. Which, if any, do you consider to be 'exotic'? Are there any that you don't know the name of, or what they taste like? Can you, for example, tell the difference between a plantain and a banana? Do you know where they come from, or the way in which they would have been transported to your local area?

COMPARE . . .

— When you next work on this section of the text, compare your experiences of the supermarket with Jordan's account of the pineapple. What 'natural' fruits and vegetables do you understand to be 'exotic'? Rewrite a section of the novel replacing 'pineapple' with the fruit or vegetable you regard as 'exotic'. How does it alter the text for you?

CONCEPTUALISE . . .

— Use this exercise as a springboard to conceptualise your idea of what it means to be 'exotic'. Does it simply mean 'tropical', or is it a more sophisticated concept? If something is 'exotic' do we regard it as 'unnatural'? Do we desire the exotic? Does our unfamiliarity make us fearful? Would you cook a vegetable if you did not know what it tasted like?

EXTEND . . .

— When you have formed an understanding of what it means, conceptually, to be 'exotic', develop your analysis to think about individuals and communities, as well as objects. Is the 'witch' (p. 105) 'exotic' because she is unknown and 'unnatural'? Look at the treatment of the Dog-Woman's clitoris, it is described as an 'orange' (p. 106). Does this make her body exotic?

Looking over 1649

QUESTIONS FOR DISCUSSION OR ESSAYS

1. How is time made into a theme of this novel?

2. Consider and assess the development of the character of the Dog-Woman.

3. What role does Fortunata play a) in relation to the character of Jordan, and b) in relation to the themes of the novel as a whole?

4. Discuss the significance of allusion and revision in *Sexing the Cherry*.

5. Winterson's writing has been described as 'simple prose'. Do you agree?

SOME YEARS LATER
SECTION 1 (pp. 113–21)

Focus on: symbols

EVALUATE . . .

— Communication takes many forms, as the novel's use of

paintings suggests. Think about the non-linguistic forms of communication employed in the text.
— Throughout the novel the chapters are divided by symbols. Who does the banana represent, and whose voice is prefaced by the pineapple?

LIST . . .
— When you have attributed a narrative voice to the symbols list, ask yourself what you associate with these symbols. What does the banana signify? Does it represent masculinity? Is it a threat – if the banana represents the penis then what is suggested in the threat that you could eat it?

RE-EVALUATE . . .
— Look at the symbols you are presented with in this section. Why are the fruits cut? Draw evidence from the body of the text to support your understanding of the symbols.

Focus on: histories

RESEARCH . . .
— Read the section, paying particular attention to the historical figures it places in the foreground. Choose one of the icons cited and research their biography by looking them up in a dictionary of history, or on the Internet. Try to find relatively succinct resources, such as encyclopaedias, and compare and contrast the history you have discovered with the one you are given in the novel.
— Perform a close reading where you examine the differences between the account you have found and the one you are given. Do they contain the same information? What kind of language is the information presented in here? Would you describe it as formal or colloquial, jokey or serious? Which phrases do you notice to be particularly unusual in Winterson's account, and why?

ANALYSE . . .

— Use your close reading as the basis for thinking about the construction of narratives and histories. It is not only the information you are given, but also how it is presented, that influences our understanding of history.

— What kind of history is being constructed in this section? Why are these particular historical figures chosen, what connects them and what is excluded?

SOME YEARS LATER
SECTION 2 (pp. 121–9)

Focus on: characterisation

ESTABLISH . . .

— This section opens with 'I am a woman going mad' (p. 121). Use this narrative to consider the construction of character in this novel. The questions below are designed to help you with your analysis. You may choose to focus on one or two of them, or to allocate them and pool your responses.

- Who is the 'I'?
- Whose voice is deployed through the 'I' in this text?
- You may want to start by attempting a character analysis – but are you given a physical description?
- How difficult is it to describe someone's character when they tell you about their fantasies – we, as readers, may feel close to the 'I' but are we able to describe them as a person?
- Think about the connection between the 'I' that we've met here and the novel's other narrators. Are the Dog-Woman and this narrator the same character?

Remember to justify your responses with textual evidence. Point to particular features or allusions that make connections.

SOME YEARS LATER
SECTION 3 (pp. 129–34)

Focus on: myth

COMPARE . . .
— Focus on the myth of Artemis as presented here (pp. 131–4). Find another version of the story in a book of classical mythology and compare it with Winterson's version. Think about how the myth functions in terms of the novel as a whole. Why, for example, is this entitled 'Fortunata's Story'? Why is it not 'Artemis's Story'? What are the thematic connections linking Fortunata and Artemis?

EXTEND . . .
— Think about why this myth is central to the text. Which narratives does it mirror? Which does it play upon? Remember to include material from this section as a whole. Think about the theme of murder and the female as a sexual object – where else can we, as readers, identify these themes?

SOME YEARS LATER
SECTION 4 (pp. 134–8)

Focus on: the Hopi

PONDER . . .
— Here Jordan and his mother discuss his encounter with the 'Hopi' (pp. 134–5). The Hopi tribe were investigated and

reported by two anthropologists Sapir and Whorf. The anthropologists argue that the tribe demonstrates how language frames the universe. Their version of the world is incomprehensible to us because they have no concept of the past or the future. It does not exist for them.

— Sapir and Whorf argue that we comprehend the world around us through language. Language frames understanding and not the other way around. Before you continue with your analysis, stop and think about this philosophy. Talk through its implications – is it a version of the power of language that is familiar to you?

COMPARE AND ASSESS . . .

— If you look at the interview with Winterson you will see that she speaks about time and about the significance of the present on p. 24. She also speaks about using fiction to understand the world. How does this version of her ideas compare with the fictional representation she has given them in *Sexing the Cherry*?

FRAME . . .

— Look back to the opening page of the text at Winterson's other account of the Hopi tribe (p. 8). Why do you think the author opens and closes the text with a reference to this tribe?

— Look closely at the understanding she gives you of their language, how is this version of the power of language reinforced in the novel?

SOME YEARS LATER
SECTION 5 (pp. 138–44)

Focus on: the finite

SELECT AND INTERPRET . . .

— Work your way through the final pages of this novel and select the various ways in which the novel refuses to 'end'.

— How many different stories throughout the novel do not have a 'happily ever after'?

— Where are the characters when the reader sees them for the last time – are they static, individual and separate, or are they left in constant motion?

— How does the text disrupt 'time' and 'history'? Which events happen out of sequence, for example? How can a fire be started hundreds of years after it finished?

— In what ways does the text's emphasis upon journeys not taken undermine the idea that there is a single voyage at the end of the text?

EXPAND . . .

— Take your answers and use them to think about how the text destabilises the expectations of readers. Think about the refusal to end and be finite, but also how the 'I' can be more than one person or no definite character at all.

— Focus on how it is thematically disruptive – how does it distort the concepts our readings often take for granted such as:

● History
● Time
● Gender and sexuality
● Love
● Space

Add to the list as you look over the book as a whole.
— In what other ways does this book destabilise the reader?

Looking over the whole novel

QUESTIONS FOR DISCUSSION OR ESSAYS

1.   Look back at the epigraph to the novel (p. 8). How does it illuminate your reading of the novel as a whole?

2.   Discuss the analysis of time presented in the novel.

3.   'A first-person narrator is always an unreliable narrator.' Discuss.

4.   How far is Winterson's history 'real' and how far is it invented?

5.   'Rage is at the centre of *Sexing the Cherry*.' Do you agree?

6.   'I don't hate men, I just wish they'd try harder' (p. 127). How is this theme worked out in *Sexing the Cherry*?

7.   Explain why the novel is called *Sexing the Cherry*.

8.   Consider the theme of the journey as played out in the novel.

9.   Assess the importance of the multiple narratives employed in *Sexing the Cherry*.

10.   Analyse the treatment of the theme of love in the novel.

Contexts, comparisons and complementary readings

Focus on: fruit

COMPARE . . .
— Read the last chapter of Marina Warner's *No Go the Bogeyman: Lulling, Scaring and Making Mock* (1998). How do the facts and fantasies that she details there help you to understand the imagery employed in *Sexing the Cherry*?

Focus on: art

RESEARCH AND COMPARE . . .
— A number of pictures are referred to in *Sexing the Cherry*. Read the opening essay from Winterson's collection called *Art Objects* (1995: Vintage, 1996). How do Winterson's ideas about art and its function in our lives help you to place her treatment of the subject in *Sexing the Cherry*?
— You will find that there are a number of essays in this collection on writing, history and gender, that may also be useful to you as nodes of comparison.

Focus on: history as an invented entity

FIND . . .
— Read the short chapter called 'Deuteronomy' from Winterson's *Oranges Are Not the Only Fruit* (1985). It is a chapter about history and how history is made, and how conventional history often distorts the individual personal view. How do Winterson's ideas, as expressed in this earlier fiction, come across in *Sexing the Cherry*?

RESEARCH AND COMPARE . . .
— Historical novels often focus, like *Sexing the Cherry*, on a time of upheaval and revolution. Two novels that you might like to use to compare with *Sexing the Cherry* are Charles Dickens's *Barnaby Rudge* (1841) set at the time of the Gordon Riots in the eighteenth century, or his *A Tale of Two Cities* (1859) which is set at the period of the French Revolution in the late eighteenth century.

Focus on: the theme of time

RESEARCH . . .
— What is time, and how does it work? We still know little about the answers to these questions. But in the last century philosophers and scientists suggested that time is altogether more mysterious than most of us imagine. Our common-sense ideas about space and time are intricate illusions. For a start, we have to abandon the idea that space has three dimensions, or that time moves constantly along a line. *Sexing the Cherry* is one of a number of novels that were published in the late twentieth century dealing with issues to do with time and how it works. It was not so much that there was any one text making this happen, but that there was a mood in the air that meant this was a common theme.

— Read Chapter One, 'Our Picture of the Universe' in *A Brief History of Time* (1988) by Stephen Hawking. This is a scientific book, but you might also wish to look at other fictional texts that deal with time as a theme: such books might include Ian McEwan's *The Child in Time* (1987) and Martin Amis's *Time's Arrow* (1991).

HOW DO YOU REACT? . . .
● 'Time is a great healer.'
● 'Time is a great deadener.'

— Which of these statements seems to you to be more true? Why? Which of them is more relevant to the impact of *Sexing the Cherry*?

LIST AND ANALYSE VOCABULARY AND PHRASES . . .
— How do we describe time? What words or phrases do we use? Refer to a dictionary of quotations or phrases to find expressions about time. What does our language say about the attitudes to time that have found their way into commonplaces? Some expressions that you could consider might include: to make time for; to waste time; to have time; to lose time; to find the time; to be in time. You will be able to think of others.
— What similar 'conventional' phrases about time can you pick out in *Sexing the Cherry*? Where, and in what circumstances, are such phrases used pejoratively, or sardonically, or playfully?

Focus on: the idea of the city and the river

COMPARE AND ASSESS . . .
— Look at the interview with Winterson where she refers to the work of the novelist and critic Peter Ackroyd on p. 23. In particular she speaks about his ideas on the Thames to be

found in his *London: A Biography* (1999) and his notion of the city in his biography of Charles Dickens. Another book of Ackroyd's that may be of interest is his novel called *Hawksmoor* (1985) which is set in London in the early eighteenth century and which – like *Sexing the Cherry* – offers a 'fake' historical language for the period and has a double-time frame, setting the past against the present. Fill out your picture of the way that history, the city and the river are used in *Sexing the Cherry* by looking at any of these books.

Focus on: allusion and reference

FIND THE OTHER TEXT . . .
— *Sexing the Cherry* is a meditation on T. S. Eliot's poem *Four Quartets* (1935–42). Several phrases in the novel are borrowed directly from the poem. Read Eliot's poem and try to find other examples where phrases and words are reused and reinterpreted in Winterson's work.
— Then read the poem again. It is a poem about time, history, forgiveness and love: 'Quick now here, now, always'. In what ways does a reading of Eliot's poem illuminate and explain the themes in *Sexing the Cherry*?

Focus on: readers and their reactions

READ AND CONSIDER . . .
— 'Fortunata's Story' about Artemis and Orion began life as a short story that Winterson published in 1988. You can find a version of the story, called 'Orion', in her collection *The World and Other Places* (Vintage, 1988).
— Here is a letter that one reader sent to Winterson at her website, along with Winterson's reply. Think about this reader's

reaction. Do you understand, sympathise or identify with it? What does this suggest about readers' reactions to Winterson's work?

Dear Ms Winterson,
I'm currently taking a Women's Literature class in college. We recently read your short story 'Orion'. We've been put into groups and it's our responsibility to discuss 'Orion'. If you wouldn't mind emailing and letting me know your thoughts before/during/or after writing 'Orion'. I understand you're extremely busy. If time permits I look forward to receiving your response. I personally enjoyed the story very much. Especially when Artemis kills Orion. What a pig he was.

Dear Girl – your email made me laugh so much I have to reply to it myself – I wrote this story in 1988 – that is 14 years ago, when you were about 2, and like you, I have no idea what I was thinking then, before, during, or after. But I'm glad you're having a good time. You see, a writer can only do their work – and if it's any good, it exists outside of time. The rest is up to the reader.

Focus on: *time and narrative structure*

RESEARCH, COMPARE AND ASSESS . . .

— One of the themes of *Sexing the Cherry* is the treatment of time: what it is, what it may be, how we create it in our imaginations, and how it creates us. Time is one of Winterson's most significant themes. In *Sexing the Cherry* she sets an historical time against the present 'now' that seems to mimic the past, so that the past catches up with the present. In one of her other novels, *Written on the Body* (1992) Winterson uses a time scale where the narrative begins in a present, looks back to a past which then catches up with the present, and then carries on as if it were a journal or a diary. In some ways Winterson's technique re-works one that appears in a number of nineteenth century novels. The best example may be Emily Bronte's *Wuthering Heights* (1847) where the tale begins in the middle of the story with Lockwood's arrival at the Grange, goes back into a past where the first Cathy and Heathcliff are children, and which then catches up with the present as Lockwood returns to meet the younger Cathy and learn about her union with Hareton.

— Try to find as many examples as you can of 'mixed' time scales. In what ways does Winterson's narrative exploit concepts of time in both the present, past and future?

Focus on: truth versus lies

ASK YOURSELF . . .

— Look again at the section on p. 81 of *Sexing the Cherry* where the story of the Flat Earth Theory appears. Compare this passage with the short chapter called 'Deuteronomy' in Winterson's *Oranges Are Not the Only Fruit*. Or, compare it with the 'Sappho' passages in Winterson's *Art & Lies* (1994). Here Sappho says 'There's no such thing as autobiography, there's only art and lies'. Consider also the things that Winterson says in the interview about making yourself into a 'fiction' as a way of approaching life on p. 12. Think about these elements and ask yourself how you would define 'fiction' in relation to the story of a person's life. Is autobiography always either 'art' or 'lies'? How do 'truths' at certain points in history turn into 'lies' at others?

The PowerBook

IN CLOSE-UP

Reading guides for

THE POWERBOOK

BEFORE YOU BEGIN TO READ . . .
— Read the interview with Winterson. You will see there that she identifies a number of themes:

- Boundaries
- Desire
- Time
- Identity
- The city
- The river

Other themes that may be useful to consider while reading the novel include:

- Life as a story
- Intertextuality

Reading activities: detailed analysis

TITLE AND MENU

EXAMINE . . .
— Remember the title of the book and look at the list of Contents, or rather the 'MENU'. Where have these headings come from? As you read the book, bear them in mind and think how they relate to the method and the themes of the fiction.

Focus on: icons

LOOK OVER AND NOTE . . .
— You will see that throughout the book there are little line drawings introducing each of the sections. As you read, notice these. Look back at them after you have read each section and consider how they help to tell the story, or draw out certain elements in the story.

If you have read Winterson's *Sexing the Cherry* (1989) you will know that a similar technique was employed there, introduced by the publishers. How differently are the images used in the two books?

CHAPTER 1, LANGUAGE COSTUMIER
(pp. 3–5)

Focus on: storytelling and openings

CONSIDER . . .
— How are you being drawn into this story? How do you know that this is the beginning? What things in this passage help you to imagine where you are?

CHAPTER 2, OPEN HARD DRIVE
(pp. 9–22)

Focus on: imagery

SEEK OUT . . .
— What different kinds of imagery are used in this passage and in what ways is it used to suggest something other than itself? Consider the tulip, for instance. Contemplate the list of names of the different varieties of tulip. Think about the live tulip that Ali collects from the hillside; think about the dried bulbs that her mother harnesses to her; think about the live tulip that can fuck the Princess. Then ask yourself, 'When is a tulip not a tulip?' (p. 9).

ASSESS . . .
— How many other sets of imagery can you find in this passage? You might consider the idea of the journey, or the quest. The Captain speaks about both of those. He also speaks about water and the aqueduct at Antioch. Another key image is that of the 'treasure' that Ali wishes to protect. List as many as you can. Consider their relevance and importance now, and keep your lists for later. Add to them whenever you come across

related ideas or concepts in terms of the imagery that is to come.

CHAPTER 3, TERRIBLE THING TO DO TO A FLOWER . . .
(pp. 25–8)

Focus on: storytelling

COUNT UP . . .
— How many elements in this exchange are to do with stories and storytelling? Pick out as many words and phrases as you can. What key ideas about stories and the ways in which they are told are included here? Make a list of all the technical phrases and look them up in a glossary of literary terms.

CHAPTER 4, NEW DOCUMENT
(pp. 31–59)

Focus on: setting

IMAGINE AND DESCRIBE . . .
— This is a story about Paris. Or rather it is the story of a story about Paris. Obviously you are told that this is Paris, but what elements – inside the text and outside the text – make you aware of the particularity of this setting? In what ways would you consider this a romanticised view of Paris, and in what ways is it a specifically personal view of Paris? Why – in terms of the themes of the book – do you think this picture of Paris may tend to be 'romantic'?

131

Focus on: imagery and narrative method

LOOK FOR . . .

Many of the connections in this section are built up with an imagery of colour (for instance) or sets of associated ideas. One example occurs on pp. 46–7 where the two Dalmatians and their red ball set up the picture that is then followed through to the 'grainy movie' and the 'red ball of desire'. Look for as many instances of such metaphoric narrative structuring as you can find. What demands does this technique make on the reader? What pleasures does it offer the reader?

Focus on: themes

INTERPRET . . .

— 'Ali', the e-writer, says that her themes are 'Boundaries. Desire'. Bear this in mind as you read the rest of the book. How are these themes played out in *The PowerBook* overall?

ASK YOURSELF . . .

— When you've read to the end of the section, ask yourself why this passage is called 'NEW DOCUMENT'.

Looking over Chapters 1–4

QUESTIONS FOR DISCUSSION OR ESSAYS

1. Explain the conceit of the powerbook in *The PowerBook*.

2. What are the key themes of the novel so far?

3. Describe the development of ANY ONE of these images: the treasure, the journey, the idea of disguise, water.

4. Consider the treatment of the theme of storytelling in the novel so far.

5. Assess the character (or characters) of Ali.

CHAPTER 5, VIRTUAL WORLD
(pp. 63–4)

Focus on: found objects

CONSIDER . . .
— This is the first time that the term 'found objects' is mentioned (p. 63). Find out what the term means in relation to certain kinds of art practice. Then assess the ways in which the text of *The PowerBook* may be assembled around the concept of the 'found object'.

CHAPTER 6, SEARCH
(pp. 67–74)

Focus on: allusion

RESEARCH AND COMPARE . . .
— This is the first of a number of interspersed stories derived from other sources and rewritten. The main elements of the tale of Lancelot and Guinevere are taken from Malory's *Morte D'Arthur* (*c.* 1471). Find a copy of this book and read the final sections that deal with the last meeting between Lancelot and Guinevere, with the death of the Queen and Lancelot leading her funeral cortège to her burial place by King Arthur. In what ways is the story taken directly from Malory? In what ways does Winterson depart from it? What technical means, to do with metaphors and imagery, make this text distinctively 'Wintersonian'?

CHAPTER 7, GREAT AND RUINOUS LOVERS
(pp. 77–9)

Focus on: storytelling and themes

DECIDE . . .

— If you recall, Ali – or the e-writer who is telling this story – said to the Married Woman that her themes were 'Boundaries. Desire' (p. 35). Find out about any one or two of the stories listed on p. 77. In what ways does that story relate to these themes?

RESEARCH . . .

— After offering the list of 'great and ruinous lovers' the text says 'There are many more. This is a list you can write yourself' (p. 77). Think about this. What stories could you add to the list?

PONDER . . .

— The narrator tells us that there are only three possible endings to the stories of 'great and ruinous lovers': 'Revenge. Tragedy. Forgiveness' (p. 78). Do you agree? Is there any other possible ending?

COMPARE . . .

— 'Boundaries and desire' are two of Winterson's key themes, as well as those of her fictional writer. Read another of her books and compare her treatment of the subject there with her treatment of the subject here. You might look at the last section 'Ruth' of *Oranges Are Not the Only Fruit* (1985) for instance, or else at the concluding sections of *Written on the Body* (1992). What concepts are returned to in *The PowerBook*? What words and phrases are repeated? Remember that it is one of Winterson's methods to repeat and revise her own phrases in her books. She says something about this in the interview.

CHAPTER 8, OPEN IT
(pp. 83–4)

Focus on: the message in a bottle

ASK YOURSELF . . .
— In what ways does the image of the message in a bottle relate to the other imagery used in the book? What does it suggest about the section that is to come?

CHAPTER 9, VIEW
(pp. 87–116)

Focus on: setting

LOOK BACK AND COMPARE . . .
— The 'real time' narrative moves to Capri. Look back at the section that was set in Paris and compare it with this. In what ways is this a 'real' portrayal of Capri? And in what ways is it a romanticised picture? Which is more appropriate to the story being told? Why might the narrator be reaching for a 'romantic' version?

Focus on: the idea of the icon

RESEARCH . . .
— Look up the meanings of the word 'icon'. What does it mean in the Russian Orthodox Church? What does it mean in literary criticism? What does it mean in the language of the

computer? What does it mean in the language of political or social analysis? Once you have a list of such meanings, ask yourself how each one might relate to the other.

— Then consider the ways in which this particular story of the events in Capri might be connected to any one (or all) of these meanings of the 'icon' idea. Look at the illustration on p. 85 that prefaces the section. Think about the idealised image of the Married Woman. Think about the story of the frisbee. Think about the idea of the island of Capri itself. Think about the story of Tiberius (p. 88) or the story of Oscar Wilde (p. 91).

Looking over Chapters 5–9

QUESTIONS FOR DISCUSSION OR ESSAYS

1. 'To err is human. To totally muck things up requires a computer.' Discuss in relation to the e-writing premise of *The PowerBook*.

2. 'The mind is a curved space' (p. 94). Consider this statement in the light of the narrative method in *The PowerBook*.

3. Explain how the interspersed stories that you have read so far relate to the main 'real time' story of the novel.

4. 'You can change the story. You are the story.' Do you agree?

5. Analyse the descriptive techniques used in setting the scene for any ONE of the places figuring in the novel so far.

CHAPTER 10, NIGHT SCREEN
(p. 119)

Focus on: narrative

ASK YOURSELF . . .
— Why do you suppose this section is so short?

CHAPTER 11, VIEW AS ICON
(pp. 123–9)

Focus on: the idea of the icon

LOOK BACK . . .
— Look back at Chapter 9 where we asked you to consider the idea of the icon. Ask yourself the same questions about this passage. Remember that that passage was called 'VIEW'. How does each one relate to the other? In what ways does the story of Paolo and Francesca figure as an icon? In what ways – in the terms of this story – does Paolo figure as an icon?

Focus on: reading

CONSIDER AND ASSESS . . .
— Why is it important that Paolo and Francesca are reading a book together when they first embark on the adulterous stage of their affair, and thereafter, as they continue it? And why is it important that they are reading 'the story of Lancelot du Lac, and his love for Queen Guinevere' (pp. 127–8). In what several ways does this inter-set story relate to the themes of *The PowerBook*, and to the themes of 'Boundaries. Desire'?

CHAPTER 12, BLAME MY PARENTS
(pp. 133–4)

Focus on: found objects

HOW? . . .
— How does this very short section relate to the continuing theme of 'found objects'?

CHAPTER 13, EMPTY TRASH
(pp. 137–46)

Focus on: narrative method and point of view

ASSESS . . .
— The tone of this passage is different from any of the earlier sections. The narrative point of view is also quite different in that the speaker positions herself as a child and gives a child's perspective while the (skewed and odd) perspectives of Mr and Mrs M are also allowed in. Read this part carefully and consider how the child's point of view changes the method of the narrative. Then ask yourself about the ways in which it may actually relate to the passages that have gone before.

Focus on: found objects and buried treasure

DISCUSS . . .
— In a group or by yourself, take these two phrases and discuss the ways in which they relate to the themes of the novel. Count up the number of times you have met these images and count up the number of different contexts in which you have found them.

Focus on: parents and children

IMAGINE . . .

— Think about your own childhood and your own relation to your parents. Try to remember how you felt about them while you were a child – as opposed to how you may feel about them now. Imagine yourself back in that past and write a short story about your relations with and feelings towards them.

CHAPTER 14, SPECIAL
(pp. 149–52)

Focus on: the themes of time and the journey

INTERPRET . . .

— How are the themes of time and time's effects on the body, and the theme of the journey played out in this chapter? What connections – in relation to either theme – can you make a) to the other inset stories in the novel (e.g., Paolo and Francesca, Lancelot and Guinevere, the tulip bearer and the Princess), and b) to the 'real time' main story in the novel?

CHAPTER 15, OWN HERO
(pp. 155–7)

Focus on: fairy tales

COUNT . . .

— How many references to fairy tales can you find in this section? What other sorts of stories are alluded to?

Focus on: the narrator

JUDGE . . .
— What is your attitude to the narrator now that you have read this section along with the previous three? How does it help you understand the narrator's drive to tell stories?

COMPARE . . .
— In Winterson's 1987 novel *The Passion*, Henri also writes and says, 'I'm telling you stories. Trust me.' If you have read that book, compare the role of the narrator there with the narrator in *The PowerBook*. Can you trust her?

CHAPTER 16, MEATSPACE
(pp. 161–2)

Focus on: language

NOTE . . .
— The conversation between Ali and the Married Woman is set up in terms of oppositions and contradictions. Work out the positive and the negative of each. How does this manipulation of vocabulary work? How many puns are used? What does this confrontational language contribute to the growing tension in the 'real time' story?

CHAPTER 17, SPITALFIELDS
(pp. 165–70)

Focus on: the city

COMPARE . . .
— If you have read Winterson's *The Passion*, look at the

opening of the section entitled 'The Queen of Spades' and assess how the descriptions of Venice may be compared with the descriptions of Spitalfields in this section.

Focus on: found objects

RECREATE . . .
— Read this conundrum.

> On the way to work one morning a man and his
> young son are involved in a car crash. The father is
> killed instantly. The child is rushed to hospital where
> it is found that his injuries are severe and that he
> needs an emergency operation. All is made ready.
> But as he is wheeled into the operating theatre the
> surgeon says, 'I can't operate on this child. He's my
> son.'

Is there a problem with this? What is the answer? If you are still puzzled, try it out on your friends until you get the solution. (Otherwise turn to the Contexts section for the answer.)
— Then read the story about the Roman sarcophagus found in the City. What is the connection?
— Then make up a similar story or 'conundrum' to bring out the same moral.

ANALYSE . . .
— How is the continuing theme of 'found objects' worked out in this section?

CHAPTER 18, HELP
(pp. 173–89)

Focus on: the quest

ANALYSE . . .

— How is the theme of the quest worked out in this section?

LOOK BACK, COMPARE AND CONSIDER YOUR POSITION
AS READER . . .

— This is the third time that Ali and the Married Woman have been together. In what ways does this episode repeat the terms of the previous two episodes? Write down as many things as you can. In all three, for instance, they share a meal and we are told what they eat. How does this repetition help to set up a memory of events for you, the reader? What role does this place you in? How critical are you of each of the lovers' actions?

ASK YOURSELF . . .

— Ali says that 'to love you calmly is not to love you at all' (p. 189). Do you agree? How far is that the proposition of all the stories of 'great and ruinous lovers' included in this book?

Focus on: narrative method

WHY? . . .

— For the first time Ali tells an 'inset story' – the story of the Princess and the fox (pp. 179–81) within one of the 'real time' sections. Why does it happen here? What is the implication in terms of the narrative method? Also, why is the recipe included here (pp. 182–3)? What does this suggest about narrative shaping and storytelling?

HOW? . . .

— 'Fragments, hints, clues, letters, persuade me on' (p. 188).

In what ways is this an apposite description of the storytelling method and the themes of *The PowerBook*?

CHAPTER 19, SHOW BALLOONS
(pp. 193–6)

Focus on: the treasure

CONSIDER . . .
— In what ways does this section on the Muck House add to the theme of the 'buried treasure'? Why is the key 'waiting for the door' (p. 196)?

CHAPTER 20, CHOOSER
(pp. 199–206)

Focus on: endings or beginnings

ASK YOURSELF . . .
— What do you think happens at Paddington Station (pp. 205–6)?

MAKE UP . . .
— Look at the (revised) story of what happens when the chosen people arrive at the Promised Land (pp. 200–1). They decide to turn away from it because it's just too much to take and settle for the Wilderness they know. Make up a similar joke story about how people desire something, but then find it is too much and turn away. Think about this saying: 'The gods punish us with what we ask for.' Is this too cynical about human aspiration? What do you think is more important: the known or the unknown? The familiar or the risk?

143

CHAPTER 21, STRANGE
(pp. 209–10)

Focus on: 'reading the story'

EXPLAIN . . .
— The narrator says, 'I'm sitting at my screen reading this story. In turn, the story reads me' (p. 209). Make sense of this conundrum.

CHAPTER 22, QUIT
(pp. 213–17)

Focus on: Ali

LOOK BACK . . .
— Reread the first section where Ali and his bulbs are introduced (pp. 9–22). How does this later episode, concluding the story of Ali, relate to the first?

Focus on: stories

COMPARE . . .
— First of all, compare Ali's position with that of the painter Rembrandt, as explained in this section. In what ways is Rembrandt's art compared with that of Ali? Write down as many points of connection as you can. Remember that 'boundaries' and 'disguise' will be among them.
— Then read Jeanette Winterson's short story 'Turn of the World'. It is in the collection called *The World and Other Places* (Vintage, 1997). 'Turn of the World' is a story about the solidity of telling stories, much as Ali also has stories which are solid. Compare the arguments and methods of the two texts.

CHAPTER 23, REALLY QUIT?
(pp. 221–3)

Focus on: the moral of the treasure

WHAT DOES IT MEAN? . . .
— What does this story and its conclusion suggest to you?
What moral might you draw from it?

Focus on: yourself

THINK ABOUT IT . . .
— Do just that.

CHAPTER 24, RESTART
(pp. 227–32)

Focus on: vocabulary

EXPLAIN AND ASSESS . . .
Chapters 23 and 24 both begin with the words 'The Map. The
Treasure' (pp. 221, 227). Look over this section and check how
many words and phrases that you have already met are included
here. The idea of the 'Wilderness' is one. Find as many others
as you can. Then work out the ways in which each of these
occurrences might relate to each of the others. Allow yourself
to be as wildly imaginative as you can. What does this poetic
network of images suggest about the nature of the narrative
method? And how does it relate to the overall theme of 'found
objects'?

CHAPTER 25, SAVE
(pp. 235–44)

Focus on: stories

COUNT . . .

— How many stories can you find mentioned in this section? Note them down as you read. If you don't know about the story, find out about it. How many are real? How many are fictional? For the purposes of this narrative, does it matter?

WHY? . . .

— Again an 'inset' story occurs inside the 'real time' story. Read the tale of Orlando on pp. 237–41. In what ways can you use this story to reflect on the events and themes of the novel as a whole?

Focus on: found objects

ARGUE FOR . . .

— Explain why it is fitting that the novel ends on a mudbank in the Thames. How is the continuing theme of the 'buried treasure' and of 'found objects' worked out here? Why is it important that the story concludes with a river? (If you look at the interview with Jeanette Winterson you will see that she discusses this.) How many of the themes of the book are drawn together in this closing section? Your list might include time, reading, storytelling. What else can you add?

TELL ME . . .

— What do you think happens beyond the ending of the book? Anything? Or nothing?

Looking over the whole novel

QUESTIONS FOR DISCUSSION OR ESSAYS

1. Describe the key character of the narrator of *The PowerBook*.

2. Analyse the treatment of time in the novel.

3. What is the purpose and function of the inset stories in *The PowerBook*?

4. Consider the imagery associated with ONE of the following: the river, the 'buried treasure', the 'found object', the tulip, the city, the PowerBook.

5. If you had one question to ask that could be answered by *The PowerBook* what would it be? Why would you choose it? How would Winterson's fiction answer it?

Contexts, comparisons and complementary readings

Focus on: the Web

RESEARCH, ASSESS AND CONSIDER . . .

— Think about the way that you use the Internet. What search engines do you use? What key words might you use and how do you refine a search? Are you pleased when you find what you are looking for? How much do you find that is useful, and how much of it is dross? How much of your time on line is spent looking for information and how much of it is spent looking for interaction?

— When you have jotted down some answers to these questions, think again about the construction of the metaphor in *The PowerBook*. How many of your own ideas or needs are answered by the fictions that you encounter there? How much overlap is there between the imaginative version of the Web in the fiction, and in the cyberspace version? Consider the methods, the metaphors, the images, and the practicalities.

— Then ask yourself about the strengths of the Web as an image and a form in fiction. Where do the strengths lie?

THINK ABOUT THE LABYRINTH . . .

— The 'Web' is called so because of its relation to a spider's web. Research some Classical stories of Greek mythology. For instance, the story of Arachne, the story of Ariadne and the Minotaur, the story of Penelope and the story of Philomela. All of these are tales to do with women, and power, and sexual relations. They are usually also to do with telling stories.

— When you have read some of these stories assess the 'Web' metaphor in *The PowerBook* in terms of its persuasiveness. What mazes are we taken into? What leads are we given? What prizes are at stake?

COMPARE . . .

— In Winterson's fiction *The Passion* (1987) Venice is described as a 'city of mazes'. How might the 'maze' of Venice compare with the literary 'maze' of *The PowerBook?*

Focus on: intertextuality

RESEARCH AND COMPARE . . .

— The literary shape of *The PowerBook* works around a number of other texts which give measurements or reference points, but which are always being transformed into something else. Choose one such 'intertext'. It may be Dante's *Divine Journey* or Thomas Malory's *Morte d'Arthur*; it may be conventional fairy tales; it may be Winterson's own *Oranges Are Not the Only Fruit* (as relating to the chapters on the 'Muck House'); or it may be the history of the craze for the tulip in eighteenth century England. Whichever is the case, find out about one of these parallel stories and work out how they are re-interpreted and re-invented in *The PowerBook*.

Focus on: found objects

THE ANSWER . . .

— The answer to the conundrum posed in relation to chapter 17 is: the surgeon is a woman.

Focus on: literary experiment

RESEARCH . . .

— Winterson says in the interview that she allies herself with a European and Modernist tradition of experimental fiction on p. 19. Virginia Woolf is a writer whom she admires. Read her introduction to Woolf's novel *The Waves* in the Vintage edition (1999) and read Winterson's two essays on Woolf in her collection entitled *Art Objects*. In what ways can you trace a connection between the two writers? Look for formal prose patterns and ways of using language as well as themes.

COMPARE . . .

— There is one contemporary American writer whose work has affinities with Winterson – Kathy Acker. Read Winterson's introduction to *Essential Acker: The selected writings of Kathy Acker*, eds Amy Scholder and Dennis Cooper (Grove Press, New York, 2002, pp. vii–x) and read some of Acker's writing. In what ways might the methods that Acker uses relate to the techniques that Winterson adopts in *The PowerBook*?

Focus on: cross dressing

COLLECT AND COMPARE . . .

— Cross dressing (generally women dressing as men) figures in Winterson's *The Passion*, in *Sexing the Cherry* and in

The PowerBook. Collect examples from the texts and compare what each of the novels say on the subject. Jot down the key phrases that offer a philosophical perspective on the practice. What do they tell us about men and women and relations between them?

— If you want to learn more about the history of cross dressing in real life look up Peter Ackroyd's *Dressing up, Transvestism and Drag: the History of an Obsession* (1979) or Marjorie Garber's *Vested Interests: Cross Dressing and Cultural Anxiety* (1992).

— If you want to find other, earlier fictional examples look up and compare Shakespeare's *Twelfth Night* or *Two Gentlemen of Verona* or *As You Like It* or *The Merchant of Venice*. Alternatively, look up Charlotte Brontë's *Jane Eyre* (1847) where Rochester disguises himself as a gypsy woman, or *Villette* (1854) where Lucy Snowe acts the part of a man in the school play. You could also look at Virginia Woolf's *Orlando* (1928) where Orlando begins his four-hundred-year life as a man but turns into a woman in the eighteenth century.

Focus on: adaptation

SEE IF YOU CAN . . .

— In 2002 the National Theatre staged an adaptation of *The PowerBook* by Deborah Warner, Fiona Shaw and Winterson herself. It starred Fiona Shaw and Saffron Burrows and was directed by Deborah Warner. If you have the chance to see this adaptation on tour consider how the novel has been adapted to make a script for the stage, remembering the constraints that Winterson mentions in the interview. Think about the different ways in which the inset stories in the novel are presented on stage. Think also about what is added to the adaptation in terms of music, movement, images.

Focus on: allusion and opera

COMPARE . . .

— In Winterson's novel *Art & Lies* (1994) there are three first person narrators who are named 'Picasso', 'Sappho' and 'Handel'. None of them is a direct representation of the historical figure of that name – each is a modern re-interpretation. Read some, or all, of *Art & Lies* and think about the ways in which its themes might resemble those within *The PowerBook*. The transfiguring power of art is the overarching image, but there are many smaller connections that might also be made. Make a list.

— At the end of *Art & Lies* all three voices speak together in a trio. The very end of the novel is taken up with a reproduction of the score for the famous Act III trio that ends Richard Strauss's 1911 opera *Der Rosenkavalier*. See the opera if you can, or listen to a recording, or just read the account of the plot in Kobbe's *Guide to the Opera*. How might the themes of the opera figure in relation to the themes of *The PowerBook*? Think particularly about the flower imagery – the rose in one, and the tulip in the other. Think also about cross dressing.

Focus on: poetry

CONSIDER . . .

— Though Winterson says in the interview that she does not count herself as a poet, she does agree that she uses poetic techniques favouring structures that allow her writing a style that is 'agile' and 'quick' on p. 22. Look up two poems. The first is by the Welsh poet R.S. Thomas and is called 'The Bright Field'. Winterson chose this as one of her favourites in *Poems for Refugees* ed Pippa Haywood (Vintage, 2002). The second is 'The Thing in the Gap-stone Stile' in the collection of the

same name by Alice Oswald (Oxford University Press, 1999).
— How might either, or both of these poems, help you think about a) Winterson's style of writing and b) Winterson's themes in *The PowerBook*? Some of the things that you might like to consider in relation to this question are:

- Time
- Risk
- Perspective
- Self-analysis
- Buried treasure
- 'Be here now'.

Reference

Critical Overview

Literary critics took up Winterson's work quite early on in her career as a writer. In one way this seems appropriate because Winterson's style is particular, her vocabulary sparing and cautious, and her narrative structures are elaborate and convincing. But in fact, it was not her stylistic and formal methods that attracted critics. Rather, it was the historical convergence of her arrival on the scene, as a new writer, with the relatively early stages of a recognisable 'lesbian' criticism, growing out of the theoretical frames of feminist theory. This did cause a problem in that many of the earliest articles on Winterson's work dealt with her writings from the angle of 'lesbian theory' but failed to deal sophisticatedly with that idea. Winterson was a well-known lesbian. Therefore her works were examples of 'lesbian writing'. Therefore it was perceived that her works were ripe for 'lesbian criticism'.

Not so. Winterson is not and never has been a 'lesbian writer'. She is a writer. Only one of her titles can be read in terms of 'lesbian criticism' and that is *Oranges Are Not the Only Fruit* where the specifics of the plot do rely on the facts created by a relationship between women, and where, concomitantly, there is an attention to arguments to do with the power relations between women.

Of these early critical essays there were some that did offer a serious and attentive reading of Winterson's work. Rebecca O'Rourke's essay 'Fingers in the Fruit Basket: A Feminist Reading of Jeanette Winterson's *Oranges Are Not the Only Fruit*' is one such example, focusing on the metaphors of transgression in the novel. Hilary Hinds's 1992 essay mainly addresses itself to the television adaptation of *Oranges* but it does so with clarity and a sensitive understanding of the origins and themes of the novel itself. Rachel Wingfield's essay on 'Lesbian Writers in the Mainstream' places a label on Winterson's work which is not necessarily appropriate and which assumes that – by definition – her work is not in the 'mainstream'. However, Winterson has long since been established as a major author on the literary scene.

The theme of transgression – of many different kinds – is one that still comes up in critical writings on Winterson's work. Cath Stowers's essay 'Journeying with Jeanette: Transgressive Travels in Winterson's Fiction' is one such, but it does deal with narrative issues as well. Questions to do with 'otherness' and 'difference' are tackled intriguingly and persuasively in the works of Andrea L. Harris in *Other Sexes: Re-Writing Difference from Woolf to Winterson* (2000), Olivia Schoenbeck, *Their Versions of the Facts* (2000) and Lauren Rusk, *The Life Writing of Otherness* (2002).

Attention to the thematic structures of Winterson's work was an important departure, recognising, as it does, that it often functions around a process of comparison and analogy. The reader is expected to do the work and put the pieces back together again. Alongside this is the attention that Winterson and her works give to narrative, narrators and narrative structures. Susana Onega began this important strand of Winterson criticism with her essay "'I'm telling you stories: Trust Me'': History/Story-Telling in Jeanette Winterson's *Oranges Are Not the Only Fruit*'. It is interesting that it was the narrative shapes in *The Passion* that began this trend, but it's not surprising, as that is also a novel about a writer (Henri) and a storyteller (Villanelle).

The same impulse lies behind Judith Seaboyer's essay on *The Passion* called 'Second Death in Venice: Romanticism and the Compulsion to Repeat in Jeanette Winterson's *The Passion*'. This is a discerning essay, acknowledging Winterson's favourite methods of repetition and return – a technique that appears in all her novels, not just *The Passion*. Narrative – its shapes, routines, voices and tones – the main subject of some of the best work on Winterson, including parts of the book edited by Helena Grice and Tim Woods, Christopher Pressler's privately published book, and the collection of essays edited by Bengtson, Børch and Maagaard. This last collection of essays offers by far the most comprehensive and intelligent assessment of Winterson's work and the diversity of essays is heartening. It is not surprising that this is a European publication – produced in Scandinavia – given that Winterson's literary ancestors are distinctively allied with European traditions in experimental writing.

A relatively early essay on Winterson dealt with her treatment of romantic love – Lynne Pearce's '"Written on Tablets of Stone": Jeanette Winterson, Barthes, and the Discourse of Romantic Love'. Given that love is one of Winterson's major themes, returned to again and again, Pearce's is a persuasive essay that places the fiction within an academic discourse on romantic love. If anything, Winterson's later works – especially *Written on the Body* (1992) – make it clear that this is a subject for criticism that could do with yet more examination.

Following on from this theme, two more recent books take up Winterson's literary function as a high priestess of feeling. These are Carolyn Allen's book *Following Djuna: Women Lovers and the Erotics of Loss* (1996) and Leigh Gilmore's *The Limits of Autobiography: Trauma and Testimony* (2001). The titles speak for themselves.

There is no doubt that Winterson's work serves for many as a memorialising text. One of Winterson's fans had 'Why is the measure of love loss?' printed on the funeral card for their beloved. What this suggests is the ways in which Winterson criticism has moved on. From a ghettoisation in the 'lesbian bylines' Winterson has come to be recognised as the kind of writer that she really is. Her formal methods with narrative and structure are noticed and analysed; her vocabulary and play with words are assessed; her images of the journey, or the concepts of transgression and 'crossing over' are examined; her great themes of love, desire, loss, boundaries, time, and identity are being treated with the seriousness they deserve.

One important development for critics and readers is the new availabilities of the Internet. Winterson runs her own official website and the address is given in the Select Bibliography. But in addition there is a readers' website run by Anna Troberg. Here you can find bibliographies, critical assessments and message board chats with other Winterson fans. The address is given in the Contexts section for *Oranges Are Not the Only Fruit*.

A great number of postgraduate students are presently writing their theses on Winterson; a greater number of undergraduates write essays on her work; an even greater number read her work at school. Winterson's readership grows day by day. So does the Winterson scholarship. Just as the trends covered in those works expand, so the reception for Winterson's work will expand.

(All of the titles of critical works are listed in the Bibliography at the end of this book.)

Selected extracts from reviews

These brief extracts from contemporary reviews of Winterson's work are designed to be used to suggest angles on the text that may be relevant to the themes of the books, their settings, their literary methods, to their historical contexts, or to indicate their relevance to issues, questions or problems today.

Sometimes one reviewer's opinion will be entirely contradicted by another's. You might use these passages to ask yourself whether or not you agree with the writer's assessments. Or else you may take phrases from these reviews to use for framing questions – for discussion, or for essays – about the texts.

The following extracts have been chosen because they are sensible and discerning. Remember though two things about newspaper reviews. They are often written under pressure; and they have to give the reader some idea of what the book under discussion is like, so they do tend to give space to summarising the plot.

None of these critical opinions are the last word. They are simply contributions to a cultural debate. As such, they should be approached with intellectual interest – because they can give the mood and tone of a particular time – and they should be treated with caution – because the very fact of that prevailing mood and time may distort a clear reading.

Lorna Sage
From the *Times Literary Supplement*, 17 June 1994
On style, priorities and method

One of the book's [*Art & Lies*] main charms is the
way it casts the brute real as the stuff you have to
smuggle in – the illicit 'lie'. While the flights of
fancy, the quotations, the pastiche and parody, the
fake aphorisms, the impossible anecdotes, the made-
up and embroidered and luxurious and libidinous
'extras' are the text's bread-and-butter pudding, its
paradoxical ballast – 'the real solid world of images'.
We are now licensed to make it up as we go along,
high up over that stage, balancing on 'the girders of
the imagination'.

Laura Cumming,
From the *Guardian*, 3 September 1992
On language and images

Winterson is always fearless in her secular appropria-
tions from religion – the hymn, the parable, the
sermon. In a series of anatomy lessons which lay
out the pathology of cancer, the narrator creates a
love poem to Louise which begins with the desire to
enter her blood-stream, and ambush the tyrannical
cells, and rises to a Solomonic song ...

Perhaps the finest passage in the book [*Written on
the Body*] comes as the narrator expresses hope in the
image of an early saint, setting out in a poor coracle
across the icy ocean praying for an uncharted place
to raise a new cathedral.

Teresa Waugh
From the *Spectator*, 9 September 2000
On the fun

The sparkling originality of Jeanette Winterson's new
novel *The PowerBook* is all the more enjoyable for
being, despite its extraordinary flights of fantasy and
a rich mixture of literary and historical references,
entirely unpretentious ...

This reviewer for one was as delighted by
Winterson's recipe for tomato sauce as by her list of
great and ruinous lovers which rates Burton and
Taylor, Oscar and Bosie alongside the likes of
Tristan and Isolde and Paolo and Francesca ...

Winterson never seems to put a foot wrong. You
can sometimes feel her sailing dangerously near the
wind as she scurries along, tacking between sixteenth
century Turkey, the mythical world of Lancelot and
Guinevere and present day Italy, talking of love and
power and the Net, but she miraculously manages
never to fall into sentimentality, banality, or tenden-
tiousness of any kind.

Kate Kellaway
From the *Observer*, September 2000
On themes

Love is Jeanette Winterson's subject – or the only
one to which she has been faithful. Sometimes her
writing about love has been fey and pretentious (I
could not get on with *The Passion* with its cute
Napoleonic posturing), sometimes brave and true
(*Written on the Body* was an extraordinary extended

love letter). There is something gallant about Winterson's persistence – she has never been a faint-hearted romantic. She has never stopped trying to unriddle love. *The Passion*, *Sexing the Cherry*, *Written on the Body* are all romantic crusades. And Winterson's lesbian identity is essential to this: she writes with the zeal of a St George liberating a princess from the dragon's mouth.

Indeed, *The PowerBook* reads more than anything like a rescue operation.

She is resolved to salvage love from everything that endangers it. But she knows it is a refrain: 'There is no love that does not pierce the hands and feet'. The Christian overtone recalls Oscar Wilde's *The Selfish Giant* and although her wit is not Wildean (it is all her own), she does share his romantic quasi-religious morbidity. She knows what lovers are up against.

Lucy Hughes-Hallett
From the *Guardian*, September 1992
On the first person

It is a love story [*Written on the Body*] with only one character, and that one elusive. We share the narrator's viewpoint, emotions past and present and a stock of remembered or imagined images, but we do not know his or her sex. The withholding of this piece of information is easily accomplished. (The speaking subject is always grammatically androgynous: 'I' is always an ungendered pronoun. Sexual difference exists linguistically only in the third person, in the eye of the beholder who says 'he or she'.) The result is a subtle blend of intimacy and mystification. It is virtually impossible to visualise a person without assigning a gender to it. We cannot see the character to whose consciousness we are allowed so close, anymore than we can see ourselves. Reading this novel is like living in a house without mirrors.

Glossary of literary terms

Allusion Where deliberate mention is made of some other literary text, cultural phenomenon, or historical fact.

Anagram Used extensively in crossword puzzles where the same letters are used to spell two different words, ideas or whatever. In this case consider the example of the near anagram of 'Jeanette Winterson', as against 'Winnet Stonejar'.

Autobiography Where the story of a life of an individual is told by that person themselves.

Bathos Deriving from the Greek word for 'depth' and signifying the opposite of 'sublime' which deals with 'loftiness' or high flown sentiments or concepts.

Cliché A phrase, idea or term that is so familiar that it has no 'cutting edge' any more.

Direct speech Where the speech of the speaker is represented as it was actually said. 'Do you want to go now?' he said. As opposed to indirect speech, 'He asked if I wanted to go.'

Double narrative Two styles make up the structure of the narrative, or two narrators with different voices tell the story.

Fairy stories Literally a tale told about or by fairies – 'Les Contes des Fées' in French – but from the eighteenth century on, when many oral stories came to be collected and written down, a story that has many incarnations but is often formulaic, and that will begin with a patterned opening – 'Once upon a time' – and end in some predictable way – 'and they all lived happily ever after'. If such stories do not have a moral content, they very often do have some social agenda.

First person narrative When the narrative is told through the eyes of one character, using the pronoun 'I'.

Imagery Literally, to do with pictures in written representation, but, in effect, any figure of speech that imaginatively represents one thing as something it is not.

Incongruity Where something is, strictly speaking, inappropriate in the context.

Indirect speech 'He told me that the earth was flat', as opposed to direct speech 'The earth is flat'.

Intertextuality The name given to the practice of artistically invoked reference to another key text. So, for instance, John Milton's *Paradise Lost* is a work intertextually linked with the Bible.

Juxtaposition One thing set against another.

Literal According to the letter.

Magic realism A much misused term often employed in relation to the 'magic' and forgetting the 'realism'. It grew out of a particular strand developing from the 1960s on where 'magic' events would occur in settings that were detailed and 'realistic' in the old fashioned sense of the Victorian realist novel which sets out to pretend that events being described are – in some sense – a history. In fact, all literature is effectively 'magic' in that it is not real, and all literature is effectively 'realistic' in that it comes from the mind of one person and enters the mind of another. An example of this style might be Angela Carter's novel *Nights at the Circus* (1986) which is set in late Victorian London and describes that scene minutely, but where we are to believe simultaneously that the heroine was hatched out of an egg and has wings.

Metaphor Any figure of speech by which one thing is explained or described by relating it to some other thing. It splits into two elements: the 'tenor' which is the primary subject, and the 'vehicle' which is the secondary figurative term applied to it. For instance, in 'the whirligig of time', 'time' is the 'tenor' or the primary subject because the metaphor is designed to tell us something about the nature of time, and the 'whirligig' is the 'vehicle' because it is the image or figure designed to show what time is like.

Narrative methods The ways in which a story is told, or the ways in which a text is presented.

Parable A story with some kind of moral or socially control-ling element.

Sublime An attitude, fact, or feeling of awesomeness and grandeur in nature or in art. Many eighteenth-century writers, thinkers and artists investigated the term as a result of the renewed popularity of an anonymous first-century AD. treatise *Perishypsous on the Sublime* attributed to Longinus. The most important work was Edmund Burke's *Philosophical Enquiry into the Origin of Our Ideas of the Sublime and the Beautiful* (1757).

Surreal Something above or beyond realism. So not 'real' at all.

Symbol A thing that stands for another thing.

Third person 'He', as opposed to 'I'.

Villanelle An elaborate, poetic stanza form consisting of five tercets (three lines) rhyming aba and a quatrain (four lines) rhyming abaa, and with regular repetition of lines 1 and 3 of the first tercet. Dylan Thomas's poem 'Do not go gentle into that good night' (1952) is an example of a villanelle.

Biographical outline

1959 27 August: Jeanette Winterson born. Adopted by Constance and John William Winterson.

1970–81 Educated at Accrington Girls' Grammar School, Accrington College of Further Education and St Catherine's College, Oxford.

1984 Worked at the Roundhouse Theatre and Pandora Press.

1985 *Oranges Are Not the Only Fruit* and *Boating for Beginners* published. Won Whitbread First Novel Award for *Oranges Are Not the Only Fruit*.

1986 *Fit for the Future* published.

1987 *The Passion* published. Won the John Llewelyn Rhys Prize for *The Passion*.

1989 *Sexing the Cherry* published. Won the E. M. Forster Award (American Academy and Institute of Arts and Letters).

1990 *Oranges Are Not the Only Fruit* made into a TV drama. This won a BAFTA for Best Drama and the Prix d'argent for Best Script.

1992 *Written on the Body* published.

1994 *Art & Lies* published. The screenplays *Great Moments in Aviation* and *Oranges Are Not the Only Fruit* published.

1995 *Art Objects* published.

1997 *Gut Symmetries* published.

1998 *The World and Other Places* published.

1999 Won the Mantua Festival International Fiction Prize for Experimental Literature.
2000 *The PowerBook* published.
2003 *The King of Capri* and *Weight* published.

Select bibliography

WORKS BY JEANETTE WINTERSON

Oranges Are Not the Only Fruit (Pandora Press, London, 1985; Vintage, London, 1991)

Boating for Beginners (Methuen, London, 1985; Vintage, 1990)

Fit for the Future (Pandora Press, 1986)

The Passion (Bloomsbury, London, 1987; Vintage, 1996)

Sexing the Cherry (Bloomsbury, 1989; Vintage, 1990)

Written on the Body (Jonathan Cape, London, 1992; Vintage, 1993)

Great Moments in Aviation and *Oranges Are Not the Only Fruit*, screenplays (Vintage, 1994)

Art & Lies (Jonathan Cape, 1994; Vintage, 1995)

Art Objects (Jonathan Cape, 1995; Vintage, 1996)

Gut Symmetries (Granta, London, 1997)

The World and Other Places (Jonathan Cape, 1998; Vintage, 1999)

The PowerBook (Jonathan Cape, 2000; Vintage, 2001)

The King of Capri, a story for children (Bloomsbury, 2003)

Weight (Canongate, Edinburgh, 2003)

INTERVIEWS

Audrey Bilger, 'Jeanette Winterson: The Art of Fiction', in *Paris Review*, Vol. 145 (Winter, 1997–98), pp. 68–112.

Eleanor Wachtel, 'Eleanor Wachtel with Jeanette Winterson', in *Malahat Review*, Vol. 118 (Spring, 1997), pp. 61–73.

CRITICAL WORKS

Carolyn Allen, *Following Djuna: Women Lovers and the Erotics of Loss* (Indiana University Press, Bloomington Indiana, 1996), pp. 46–80. [Includes an essay on *Written on the Body*.]

Eds Helene Bengtson, Marianne Børch, and Cindie Maagaard, *Sponsored by Demons: The Art of Jeanette Winterson* (Scholar's Press, Agedrup, 1999). [The most sophisticated collection of essays on Winterson's writing.]

Leigh Gilmore, *The Limits of Autobiography: Trauma and Testimony* (Cornell University Press, Ithaca and London, 2001), pp. 120–42 [Includes a chapter on *Written on the Body*.]

Eds Helena Grice and Tim Woods, *'I'm telling you stories': Jeanette Winterson and the Politics of Reading* (Rodopi, Amsterdam, 1998).

Andrea L. Harris, *Other Sexes: Re-Writing Difference from Woolf to Winterson* (State University of New York Press, Albany New York, 2000).

Hilary Hinds, '*Oranges Are Not the Only Fruit*: Reaching Audiences Other Lesbian Texts Cannot Reach', in ed. Sally Munt, *New Lesbian Criticism* (Harvester Wheatsheaf, Hemel Hempstead, 1992), pp. 153–72. [On the reception of the television adaptation.]

Susana Onega, '"I'm Telling You Stories. Trust Me": History/Story-Telling in Jeanette Winterson's *Oranges Are Not the Only Fruit*', in ed. Susana Onega, *Telling Histories: Narrativizing History, Historicizing Literature* (Rodopi, Amsterdam, 1995), pp. 135–47.

Rebecca O'Rourke, 'Fingers in the Fruit Basket: A Feminist Reading of Jeanette Winterson's *Oranges Are Not the Only Fruit*', in ed. Susan Sellers, *Feminist Criticism: Theory and Practice* (Harvester Wheatsheaf, Hemel Hempstead, 1991), pp. 57–70.

Lynne Pearce, '"Written on Tablets of Stone"?: Jeanette Winterson, Barthes, and the Discourse of Romantic Love', in ed. Suzanne Raitt, *Volcanoes and Pearl Divers: Essays in Lesbian Feminist Studies* (Onlywomen Press, London, 1994).

Christopher Pressler, *So Far So Linear: Responses to the Work of*

Jeanette Winterson (Paupers' Press, Nottingham, 1997).

Lauren Rusk, *The Life Writing of Otherness: Woolf, Baldwin, Kingston and Winterson* (Routledge, and Taylor and Francis, New York and London, 2002). [Includes a chapter on *Oranges Are Not the Only Fruit.*]

Olivia Schoenbeck, *Their Versions of the Facts: Text und Fiktion in der Romanen von Iain Banks, Kazuo Ishiguro, Martin Amis und Jeanette Winterson* (Wissenschaftlicher Verlag, Trier, 2000).

Judith Seaboyer, 'Second Death in Venice: Romanticism and the Compulsion to Repeat in Jeanette Winterson's *The Passion*', in *Contemporary Literature*, Vol. 38, (1997), pp. 483–509.

Cath Stowers, 'Journeying with Jeanette: Transgressive Travels in Winterson's Fiction', in eds Mary Maynard and June Purvis, *(Hetero)sexual Politics* (Taylor and Francis, London, 1995), pp. 139–58.

Rachel Wingfield, 'Lesbian Writers in the Mainstream: Sara Maitland, Jeanette Winterson and Emma Donoghue', in ed. Elaine Hutton, *Beyond Sex and Romance? The Politics of Contemporary Lesbian Fiction* (The Women's Press, London, 1998), pp. 60–80.

The editors

Jonathan Noakes has taught English in secondary schools in Britain and Australia for fifteen years. For six years he ran A-level English studies at Eton College where he is a house-master.

Margaret Reynolds is Reader in English at Queen Mary, University of London, and the presenter of BBC Radio 4's *Adventures in Poetry*. Her publications include *The Sappho Companion* and (with Angela Leighton) *Victorian Women Poets*.

Also available in Vintage

Jeanette Winterson

BOATING FOR BEGINNERS

'Winterson has re-written the Book of Genesis. Feminism and
twentieth-century kitchenware run riot in the ancient city of Ur;
Noah is Howard Hughes crossed with Frankenstein – an eccentric
overseer of thriving capitalism who makes "God" by accident out
of a piece of gateau and a giant electric toaster. The result is a
tetchy, omnipotent ice-cream cone who decides to drown all the
decadence of Winterson's world in a flood – out of which, of
course, a more fitting myth can be born, ie. that God is a benevo-
lent old man with a white beard who loves us all.'
Time Out

'If you find the Monty Python *Life of Brian* amusing, this is your
comic book of revelations'
Times

V

VINTAGE

Also available in Vintage

Jeanette Winterson

ART & LIES

'If we want language to be handled with vitality and suppleness, if we want to consider serious questions of philosophy, art and sexuality, if we want writers to aspire to beauty, then we should be glad of Jeanette Winterson ... she is a writer who will continue to astonish, to please and to vex, *Art & Lies* does all these things'
Literary Review

'The book is characterised, like all Winterson's work, by a mixture of beautiful writing, shaped line by line into word sculptures, and the kind of moral political denunciation of the crasser aspects of modern life that has helped her to be seen as a prophet of the late twentieth century'
Independent

'Winterson's belief in love, beauty and most of all, language, is evangelical and redemptive ... it is timely and exciting to read'
Times

V

VINTAGE

Also available in Vintage

Jeanette Winterson

THE WORLD AND OTHER PLACES

'A greatly gifted and original writer . . . There is an exhilarating freshness and energy to this collection . . . "Turn of the World" imagines four islands named for, and composed of, the four elements, earth, air, fire and water . . . she simply describes her imaginary islands, and in the process conveys with precision her love for the natural world, her fascination with the legends of the past her belief in the power of language and storytelling'
Observer

'An awesome panorama . . . compelling and wild . . . This is a collection that shows what an original and thrilling writer Winterson can be . . . the title story is told by a man who in childhood dreamed up fantasy flight-paths to foreign lands. He becomes a pilot, then a lone aviator. This short-haul flight of fancy is a beautiful, perfect story that shows Winterson at ease across her imaginative landscape'
Independent

V

VINTAGE

Also available in Vintage

Jeanette Winterson

ART OBJECTS

'Winterson is in fine form in these essays about art, arguing, admonishing, infuriating, teasing ... She fights solemnly, beguilingly, for ecstasy and silence and the revival of our ability to contemplate ... She says much that is important about energy and passion. Her stalwart defence of the modern is a challenge to the barrenness and niggliness with which we live'
Observer

'These essays are as comfortable, as perfect in their peculiar way, as was *Oranges* ... Remarkable'
Guardian

'A covetable volume: infuriating, stimulating'
Independent on Sunday

'There is no denying the beauty and precision of her writing, nor the clarity of her expression ... On her heroines Stein, Woolf, Eliot, books themselves, she is particularly strong and passionate. Through all, a central theme recurs: that art, true art, is and will remain a vital force, without which life is scarcely worthy of the name'
Time Out

ᐯ

VINTAGE

ALSO AVAILABLE IN VINTAGE LIVING TEXTS

❑	*Martin Amis*	0099437651	£6.99
❑	*Margaret Atwood*	009943704X	£6.99
❑	*Louis de Bernières*	0099437570	£6.99
❑	*Sebastian Faulks*	0099437562	£6.99
❑	*Ian McEwan*	0099437554	£6.99
❑	*Toni Morrison*	009943766X	£6.99
❑	*Salman Rushdie*	0099437643	£6.99
❑	*Jeanette Winterson*	0099437678	£6.99

- All Vintage books are available through mail order or from your local bookshop.
- Payment may be made using Access, Visa, Mastercard, Diners Club, Switch and Amex, or cheque, eurocheque and postal order (sterling only).

❑❑❑❑❑❑❑❑❑❑❑❑❑❑❑❑

Expiry Date:＿＿＿＿＿＿＿ Signature:＿＿＿＿＿＿＿＿＿＿＿＿

Please allow £2.50 for post and packing for the first book and £1.00 per book thereafter.

ALL ORDERS TO:
Vintage Books, Books by Post, TBS Limited, The Book Service,
Colchester Road, Frating Green, Colchester, Essex, CO7 7DW, UK.
Telephone: (01206) 256 000
Fax: (01206) 255 914

NAME: ＿＿＿＿＿＿＿＿＿＿＿＿＿＿＿＿＿＿＿＿＿＿＿＿＿＿

ADDRESS: ＿＿＿＿＿＿＿＿＿＿＿＿＿＿＿＿＿＿＿＿＿＿＿＿

＿＿＿＿＿＿＿＿＿＿＿＿＿＿＿＿＿＿＿＿＿＿＿＿＿＿＿＿＿

＿＿＿＿＿＿＿＿＿＿＿＿＿＿＿＿＿＿＿＿＿＿＿＿＿＿＿＿＿

Please allow 28 days for delivery. Please tick box if you do not wish to
receive any additional information.
Prices and availability subject to change without notice.